An Oregon Shakespeare Festival Lover's

Guide to Exploring Southern Oregon & Northern California

Written by
Louise Hays Doolittle

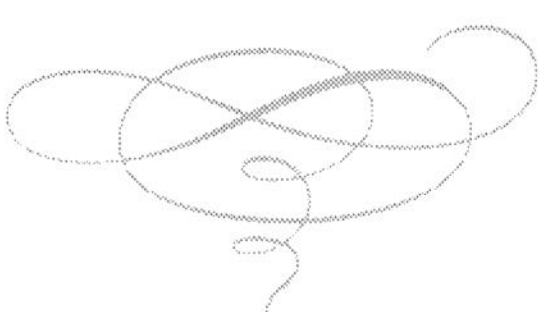

Photos by Louise Hays Doolittle
& Patty Doolittle

Library of Congress Control Number: 2013945950
ISBN-13: 9780989136068
Guide to Exploring Southern Oregon and Northern California
Second Edition 2015
Printed in the United States of America

For more information about special discounts for bulk purchases, please contact 3L Publishing at 916.300.8012 or log onto our website at www.3LPublishing.com.

Book design by Erin Pace-Molina

Contents

Photos

Animals........................ *Black Bear at Wildlife Images*

Sports .... *Table Rock Mountain for hiking*

Water Activities.............. *Four Mile Lake and fishing*

Parks in Southern Oregon .... *McKee Bridge*

Lakes... *Klamath Lake*

Rivers and Falls................................. *Mill Creek Falls*

Peaks and Mesas...................................... *Mt. Shasta*

Caves .... *Oregon Caves*

Covered Bridges .... *Lost Creek Covered Bridge*

A Day at the Beaches........................... *Oregon Coast*

Northern California............................. *Shasta Lake*

Places of Historic Interest........ *Statue of gold panner*

Wineries... *Grapes*

Food... *Wolf Creek Tavern*

Where to Get Additional Information...................
.... *Wise Owl from Wildlife Images*

Final page .... *Louise and Jim Doolittle*

Introduction

Every year thousands of people visit Southern Oregon to enjoy the Oregon Shakespeare Festival in the town of Ashland. If a visitor has only evening performances or if he's here on a Monday when the theater is dark, it's possible that the visitor will have time on his hands. This book is written to meet the needs, and perhaps the curiosity, of all visitors. Southern Oregon and Northern California are areas rich in beauty — with places to visit and pleasures to enjoy. We'll explore some of "what else there is to do" both in and out of the Festival.

For the convenience of Festival attendees and those staying in Ashland, all directions read as if Ashland was the center of the universe — all directions beginning and ending either in Ashland or Medford. A good map of the area will be helpful if not a necessity. I've found that the AAA maps are quite useful, but I'm sure there are others that would be fine.

Explanatory Note

There are a few places in this compilation of information about Southern Oregon and Northern California that describe venues or businesses that may not be in existence anymore. In fact, when I am aware of this likelihood, in some places I've said as much and told you about it anyway. So if you can't visit, why would I tell you about it?

All such places captured my interest at some time, and I want to share with you information about interesting places. Possibly you could benefit from driving past a place and remembering its history. Or perhaps you've driven past it and wondered about what it was or what its history was, and I provide the answers. In some cases, I've heard conversations indicating there are efforts being made to reinstate a place. If these efforts are successful, the place may be available when you're reading about it. With other venues, it's a surmise on my part that under some providence such a wonderful place will find supporters who will cause it to be reinstated, or maybe if enough people ask about it, a way will pop up to bring it back. In all cases, the venues are an indication of the imagination, creativity, or thoughtfulness of the citizens, and I doff my hat to them.

As noted, a few businesses have vanished. Restaurants, especially, seems to have a finite existence. Other venues change their hours. So to avoid a "CLOSED" sign, call ahead and check the hours.

What to Do – A Once-Over-Lightly

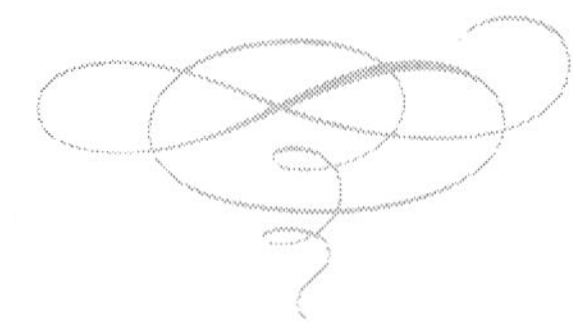

If you've come to enjoy the Festival, you know there are many things to do besides the plays. The Festival includes several non-stage activities, and another chapter will discuss those.

But perhaps you've found that you still have lots of time on your hands and are looking for other things to do. Well, you can do practically anything you're used to doing at home plus a whole lot more. In the next few pages I only touch on the possibilities. Following chapters give details for most of the venues and ideas listed below.

In Ashland itself, right next to the Festival grounds is **Lithia Park**. This is a beautiful place to stroll, people watch, throw a Frisbee or ball, read a book, knit, or take a snooze.

Can I **shop**? Of course! Ashland has several delightful small stores, and Medford additionally has many of the big-box stores. In both cities you'll find specialty shops that deal with crafting supplies, for instance — yarn, fabric, and scrapbook requirements.

Can I find a quiet place to **read**? In Ashland there are local parks besides Lithia that include shady benches. Also there are two libraries (one on Siskiyou at the end of the business district and the other on the SOU campus). At these libraries you can read or check out books, returning them before leaving town. There's also the Christian Science Reading Room in downtown Ashland (located next to the movie theater and listed in the book section of Yellow Pages in the phonebook) that has the *Christian Science Monitor* Weekly Edition plus an on-line Daily Edition for all interested. This is in addition to Bibles and denominational books and magazines.

Are there **museums**? Yes, probably every city has one in or near it. Mentioned here are some of the more interesting ones.

Ashland has the popular Scienceworks Hands-on Museum.

Additionally in Ashland, **Southern Oregon University** has a new, rather small museum. While it *is* small, the exhibits change often, providing continuing interest.

The city of **Jacksonville**, being a historic landmark, is a museum itself. Sadly, two of their museum collections have been removed to Medford, but I understand there is an effort being made to return them to Jacksonville.

Medford has an interesting library — **Southern Oregon Historical Society Historical Research Library**. This is a non-circulating institution, described as "one of the largest repositories in the Pacific Northwest," with nearly a million photographs, documents, etc. (It charges a fee and is located at 106 Central Avenue.) Medford also has a collection of museums, now in a state of flux. Check the phonebook, both for Medford and Jacksonville.

The city of **Central Point** has **The Crater Lake Museum**. Among other items at this venue are minerals from around the world, petrified wood, and American Indian artifacts. There are 30-minute guided tours available by appointment. The museum is open Tuesday through Saturday, 10:00 a.m. to 4:00 p.m. There's a fee for all visitors except those younger than 5 years of age.

Are there **covered bridges**? Yes. There are at least five within easy driving distance. Also, if you visit the AAA office on Barnett Road in Medford, they'll give members a statewide list of available bridges and their locations. Also, the Information Centers in downtown Ashland and the one by Harry and David's in Medford also provide a bridge pamphlet. Finally, Bloomsbury Book Store in downtown Ashland stocks a small book on covered bridges (*Oregon Covered Bridges* by Webber) which is very complete statewide, listing names, places, and how to get there.

Can I visit a **zoo**? Not exactly, but you can visit places where there are animals on exhibit. Four are **Wildlife Images** in Grants Pass area, **Wildlife Safari** in Winston, and **Great Cats World Park** near Cave Junction. On the coast is the fourth — the **West Coast Game Park Safari**, a petting zoo. Wildlife Safari also has a petting zoo. All these venues are discussed in the chapter on *Animals* (pp. 115).

Are there places to enjoy **sports or more athletic activities**? Yes. Below are some examples:

Can you **river raft**? Yes, white-water types or the slower, enjoy-the-sights trips. The cities of Grants Pass and Merlin are two of the starting places for such rides, but there may be others farther away. These trips may take more time or energy than you'd want to combine with an evening of Shakespeare. So, you might plan a half day of easier rafting or a whole day with no evening performances for the more strenuous rides. Reservations are recommended.

Can you **bike**? Yes, there are businesses where you can rent bikes, and there are bike paths in several locations. Though I haven't tried renting a bike, I'm sure they also will recommend where to find the paths.

What about **golf**? Yes. There are several golf courses in the area where you'll be welcome. Probably you'll want to use your own clubs, so next trip bring them with you. In the meantime a golfer friend tells me there are places that rent equipment. The Ashland golf course is Oak Knoll Golf Course, five minutes from downtown. Its contact information is: 541-482-4311 or visit the website at www.oakknoll.org. The address is 3070 Highway 66, Ashland. (Take exit 14 off I-5.)

Is **horseback riding** available? Yes, there are stables in the area where you can ride. I'm told by Ashland people who visit riding stables or own their own horses that the animals offered at these stables are fine steeds, not worn-out mounts that have seen much better days. I also understand the riding trails are very scenic. My daughter thoroughly enjoyed her ride. The Yellow Pages will help you find these stables (or check on-line).

Can you **fish**? You bet. There are several lakes and streams stocked with fish — bass, trout, and salmon — to mention a few. In fact, there's a hatchery at the southern end of Lost Creek Lake that breeds and releases fish yearly. The phone-book Yellow Pages list three shops that deal with fishing. Also, an all-purpose store at Applegate Lake and another at Howard Prairie Lake indicated recently that they sell fishing tackle if you didn't pack your own. Check locally before heading to the lakes.

Can you bring your rifles and **hunt**? Yes. Many Southern Oregonians love to hunt, and there are hunting seasons you should be aware of. Archery is also an active sport here, and folks with their bows and arrows go into the woods to hunt during certain times. If you stay on the established trails you should have no safety problems, but the end of August is a time you should check with the rangers.

Are there **hiking trails**? Absolutely. There's a Ranger Station near I-5 on the Ashland side of State 66 — on Washington, near the Arco Station. Rangers at this station will provide maps and tell you the condition of the trails. As mentioned above, you should be aware of hunting seasons, and practice wisdom in staying on the trails. Fires are too frequent a problem in Oregon, so it's always wise to check with the rangers before you set out to forested land.

Four of Jackson County Parks list hiking as one of their offerings. They are: Emigrant Lake, Howard Prairie Lake, Willow Lake, and Britt Gardens.

The City of Medford's Bear Creek Bike and Nature Trail is an 11.5-mile long path with numbered sign-posts to point out special things along the way. A wheelchair could easily navigate this path. This is located on the west side of I-5 near Table Rock Road.

What about **swimming**? Yes, not only can you swim in motel pools but in many local streams. Well, this is often more like wading (except at special places like McKee Covered Bridge Wayside), but it does cool you down. There are also several close-in lakes where you can really swim. Besides these natural venues, the Ashland YMCA offers swimming for all members (non-locals included) and allows non-members day use of their facilities (for a fee), which includes swimming. To find this YMCA, it's on the Rt. 66 drive into town from I-5. Soon after exiting the highway you'll pass an Albertson's grocery store. Just beyond this complex is a sign indicating the Y is on YMCA Road! Reverse these directions if coming from Ashland.

What about **exercising and weight lifting**? Yes, the same YMCA provides equipment for these pursuits. There are also other fitness centers and health clubs, mostly in Medford:

1. Gold's Gym – 541-779-5853
2. Power House Gym – 541-773-8564

3. YMCA in Medford – 541-482-9622

4. 24 Hour Fitness – 541-773-2454

Can I find a way of doing some **rowing**? Yes, Emigrant Lake has boats and crews working out here, and I've been told visitors are welcome. Their website is www.ashlandrowingclub.org. Check it out.

If I've not mentioned your favorite activity, explore on your own. You'll probably find it. Three helpful sources of information are the local phonebook (found in most motels or hotels), Information Centers, and of course on-line. The two closest centers are in downtown Ashland next door to the Festival's Black Swan Theater and in Medford in the small shopping center housing the Harry and David Country Store off Barnett Road.

Besides these usual pastimes, the area has a plethora of natural pleasures to entertain and awe you — lakes, waterfalls, forests, etc.

What to Do with Half a Day

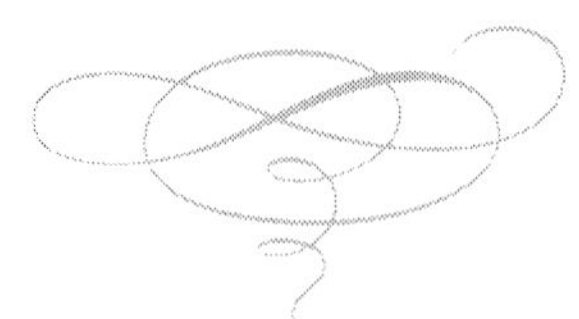

The possibilities are nearly endless. The most important things to do would be to start with the Festival. Take a backstage tour, attend a few lectures either in the park or in Carpenter Hall, or visit the Tudor Guild Gift Shop to buy Festival publications, the annual *Souvenir Program, Illuminations,* and *Prologue.* (The *Souvenir Program* includes pictures and short biographies of actors, directors, and technical staff for the season. You might want to start a collection of these if you plan to make the Ashland trip an annual event. Being able to refresh your memory about the wonderful actor you saw last year is possible with the program. *Illuminations* discusses the plays, and the *Prologue* provides interesting background for the productions.) The glass case on the edge of the bricks lists information about the events of the week.

If your time in town is limited, be sure to spend quality time in Lithia Park. It's beautiful, it's right next to the Festival, and it provides a pleasant atmosphere for strolling the easy paths.

The Scienceworks Hands-on Museum (see the chapter on *Museums,* pp. 63) is a wonderful place for exploring things related to science, and it appeals to people of all ages. Since it's right in town, you could spend as much time here as you wish.

Explore Jacksonville, 20-30 minutes from Ashland. The whole downtown is a historic area and interesting. Stopping at their Information Center, you can pick up pamphlets and maps to enhance your visit. If the trolley is running take a round-trip ride and see some of the community. Walk through the grounds of the Britt Festival, a nicely landscaped venue. Drink a sarsaparilla while strolling past the shops. If you have children with you, bring their swimsuits along and let them join other children playing in the water-play area in the city park a block from Main Street.

Timing for any of the other ideas I mention would depend on how fast you drive — always within the speed limit, of course — and how much time pleases you at the mentioned venues. Only you can gauge that, but the rest of this list is feasible.

Visit one of the area lakes to picnic and enjoy a relaxing time. (See the chapter on Lakes, pp. 165.) Another day you could pick another lake. Or if you've been to a few lakes and want something a little different, check out the local county parks for a picnic. (See the chapter on Parks, pp. 149.) At any of these places you could take a short hike, too.

If you want to go a little farther, get a little earlier start and visit one of the animal venues — Wildlife Images, Wildlife Safari, or Great Cats World Park. You could visit each one of these in about half a day, but you'd have to keep your eye on your watch to make sure you get back in time for dinner if you have theater tickets.

You could visit Oregon Caves. Since the yearlong temperature in the caves is a steady 46 degrees you may wish to carry warmer clothes with you so you won't be the one shivering.

Take a river ride. As noted in the chapter dealing with water activities, (pp. 143) there are sedate rides that take only a few hours, but they show you a lovely side of Mother Nature. Be sure to plan ahead and make a reservation if this is your choice.

Take a business tour. There's Harry and David's where they show visitors how they produce and package fine fruits and chocolates. Or tour Dogs for the Deaf and learn how they train service dogs to help the handicapped. Both of these tours are in Medford, and both require reservations.

Dip down to California to visit Yreka with its museums, historic park, and walks. Or go further south to Dunsmuir for more nature activities. You couldn't do justice to all these California places in one day, so you'd have to pick and choose.

If you got an early start so you arrive in Eagle Point by, say, 9:00 a.m., you'd be early enough to buy some of the old mill's yummy blueberry muffins. You could also enjoy their tour before returning to Ashland. In this case you'd be on time for lunch and the matinee.

There are many other possibilities discussed in this book that would be fine for half a day's activity. If you leave your hotel/motel late morning, you'd arrive around noon and could include a picnic, a short hike, etc., before returning to Ashland in the late afternoon and be in time for dinner and the theater.

What To Do with All or Most of a Day

1. **Lazy Day**. The easiest and most boring would be to do nothing but laze around your motel room. This is not recommended.

2. **Shopping**. You could spend the entire day shopping, first in Ashland and then adding Medford. This could also get boring pretty fast. This would be recommended only if you had a list of items you had to have — mandatory — before you head for home. Instead, get out and see the world.

3. **Take the Lakes Drive**. Bring your swim gear and enjoy getting thoroughly wet. Or, if you choose to not swim, sit in a chair (if you travel with one) or one of provided benches and admire the view, feel the relative cool, and get refreshed. If you have packed a lunch, there are lots of picnic tables. Drive past all the lakes listed and decide which is your favorite, one you'll want to keep visiting.

4. **Visit Crater Lake**. This is one of the wonders in the U.S. Park system. Not only is its origin remarkable, and the water is very deep, but the lake is quite beautiful. There are trails to hike (some very short), a drive to enjoy circumnavigating the lake, and even a boat ride to take. The boat ride involves a one-mile hike down to water level and then the return hike back up to your car. Outside the immediate Lake area are the **Boundary Springs**, the exciting **Rogue Gorge** and accompanying **Natural Bridges**. There are a few worthy waterfalls to enjoy after short, easy hikes.

5. **Take the waterfall drive**. Before you embark, be sure to visit a ranger station and get the map which not only locates the falls but describes them and tells how much of a hike to get to each of them. Then when you reach the highway between Diamond Lake and Roseburg, choose the falls that intrigue you the most — perhaps because of the type of falls or because of the length of hike to get to the viewing area. If you're not much of a hiker, take one or more of the falls with short hikes — they're there. Or if you enjoy hiking, you may wish to take one of the longer hikes and see fewer falls. It's your choice.

6. **Drive to the beaches**. Since the drives to the ocean are long, you'll probably want an early start. Also, allow time to stop and enjoy anything that grabs your attention along the way. I love covered bridges, and if I see one, I want to stop and enjoy it. The myrtle-wood factories are an interesting stop. (I did some Christmas shopping at one before completing the drive to the beaches.) Some communities have lovely city parks — nice for picnicking or getting out of the car to stretch your legs. (The added advantage is that they tend to have less sea breezes and therefore are warmer. Remember that you've arrived at a location much cooler than inland.) If you're an avid photographer you'll see lots of photo ops. In short, enjoy the drive as well as the destination.

7. When driving to the beaches, first do a little homework to **decide what you want to do**

once you reach the ocean. There are gardens to visit as well as lighthouses, historic sites, wharves, local industries, and tourist-oriented shops. But most of all are the beaches. They have different specialties — agate beach, shell beach, beaches with large expanses of sand, beaches near rocky outcrops, and tidal pools with exotic sea life. Some beaches are more protected than others, and if you have young children with you you'll appreciate these. One favorite secluded beach is Sunset Bay south of Coos Bay. The waves here are very gentle — just right for toddlers.

8. **Visit The Oregon Caves**. This in itself will not take the whole day, but there are other attractions in the same area: **Great Cats World Park, Kerbyville Museum, Illinois River State Park, and Selma Lake**.

9. **Drive north on I-5 to** Winston and visit **Wildlife Safari**. Drive through and see the animals roaming free within this part of the park. **If you follow the rules, you're perfectly safe because the rules insist that you stay within the safety of your car with the windows up if the animals are near.** After the drive through — or before, depending on the time — enjoy some of the animal shows presented by trainers. For additional information see Wildlife Safari in the chapter on *Animals* (pp. 115).

10. En route, just off I-5 in **Sunny Valley**, is a covered bridge—beside a small but interesting historic museum. On the way home is **Valley of the Rogue State Park**, a beautiful rest stop. It's

perfect not only for a potty break but also run-around time. If you travel with Frisbees or balls, the area is quite spacious and would accommodate a few people doing a round-robin of tossing and catching.

11. **Go hiking**. Many trails are associated with the lakes and parks (local, state, or national).

12. **Visit Jacksonville** and stroll the streets and shops. If you have young children with you don't miss the city park one block off the main street. The park has a large expanse of grass, a play area with swings and such, and a concrete-covered area with sprinklers, which is wonderful on a hot day, which would be most days, so pack the children's swimsuits.

13. **Visit Tule Lake**, a wildlife refuge, and nearby **Lava Beds National Monument**, both in Northern California on Highway 97.

14. Visit Northern California's **Yreka,** off I-5, to learn more of American Indian culture, the quest for gold, and some Mother Nature offerings. The Ranger Headquarters near I-5 — a new and lovely building — has friendly and knowledgeable staff that can give you maps or directions to the places to visit.

15. Visit Northern California off I-5 for the cities of **Mt. Shasta** and **Dunsmuir.** Both have Information Centers where you can get maps to their parks that have waterfalls. Both are fairly cool on a hot day, and lakes **Shastina** and **Siskiyou** are not far away if you want to swim.

16. Visit Northern California's **Castle Crags State Park** especially to take a short hike to enjoy the magnificent view.

Become friends with the rangers, particularly those in the Ashland Ranger Station. They're very helpful and knowledgeable.

If you've done all of the above and still have time, start at the top of the list and revisit some places you rushed through. Slow down and enjoy the small things. I remember what turned out to be an exciting day for my youngsters — toddlers and just above. We took a short nature trail and the children discovered Banana Slugs! And Redwood tree cones — who knew they were so small! And Gold-Back ferns! Without damaging the ferns we imprinted the pollen from the fern to their jeans. Ah, the adventures of slowing down!

NOTE: You've probably noticed the many times the word "hike" or a derivative is used. If you have a handicapped person with you, don't worry about this. Many of these hikes are quite short and easy. There are some places a handicapped person can enjoy from the car and other places where a wheelchair can get close enough to the attraction to feel the mist or get a lovely view, and some trails work with a chair. Trust me — "been there, done that."

City of Ashland

Ashland, Oregon — home of the renowned Oregon Shakespeare Festival and Southern Oregon University!

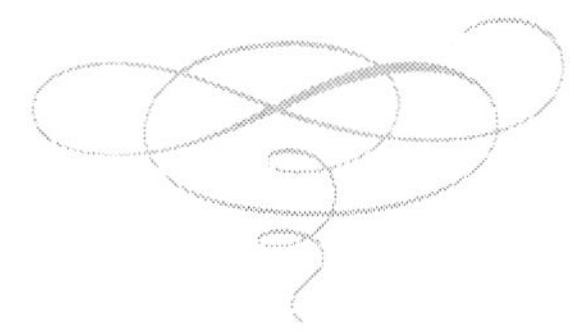

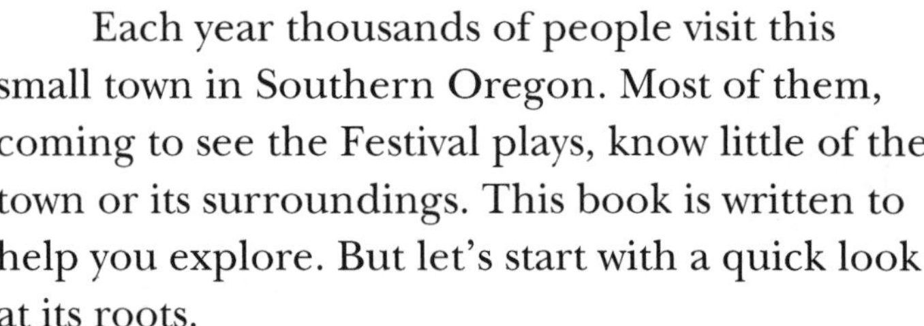

Each year thousands of people visit this small town in Southern Oregon. Most of them, coming to see the Festival plays, know little of the town or its surroundings. This book is written to help you explore. But let's start with a quick look at its roots.

Ashland's History

Like so much of the "Old" West, pioneers came here from eastern U.S., some in covered wagons. There were Indian uprisings and certainly some episodes of lawlessness and political skirmishes. The discovery of gold was important to the region, and so was the development of the railroads. Eventually Southern Oregon, especially Medford, became an agricultural center.

Most important to the early settlers of Ashland and continuing today was a love of things cultural. Ashland College (now Southern Oregon University) was established in 1872. The public library goes back to 1879. The Ganlard Opera House was built in 1889, and it served the community for a variety of uses both musical and theatrical, plus being used for such community events as graduations. This grand building has been described as the finest opera house between San Francisco and Portland. Since it's not at street level most people walk past it without noticing it.

Eighteen ninety-three marked the arrival of the popular Chautauqua, a nationwide touring group including lectures, seminars, and entertainment — even some sporting events. A dome-shaped building was built as a venue for these programs, which attracted audiences from all over Southern Oregon. That building was eventually torn down, and the Elizabethan Theater of the Shakespeare Festival was built on its site. You can still see part of the wall.

In 1935 Angus Bowmer presented the first Shakespeare Play in the Chautauqua "Tabernacle." He received permission from skeptical city fathers to present the play (*Merchant of Venice*) as a part of a July 4th celebration. They were so unsure that this would be a success that they also scheduled a boxing match — to bring in at least some money. Bowmer and his troop outsold the boxing match, and the rest is history.

When our family first started coming to Southern Oregon in the late 1960's, the area around the Festival looked very different from today. The only active Festival building was the Elizabethan Theater — pre Allen Pavilion. Where the Bowmer and Green Show bricks are now were downtown wood-frame buildings. In one of these buildings was a small theater where we attended a production of *Merchant of Venice*. A Christian Science Church occupied the building now called Carpenter Hall, and those who chose to could attend a Wednesday evening meeting and then cross the street to attend a Shakespeare play.

Not only did the festival look different, the programming was different. The slogan at that

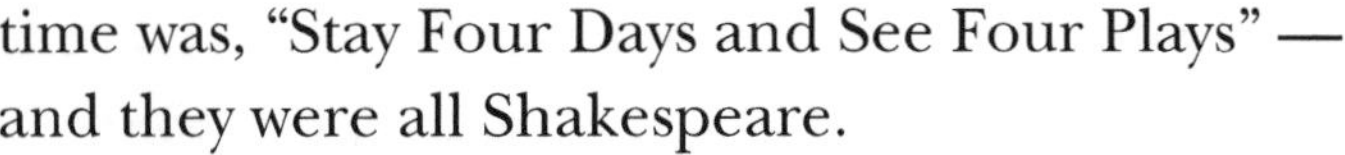

time was, "Stay Four Days and See Four Plays" — and they were all Shakespeare.

Many of the actors and "techies" then popular with the audiences have moved on to other things, and professional actors and technical crew have replaced them. True, some of these theater people earned their equity cards while working at the Festival, but many others come here already having earned their professional status. Barry Kraft and Mark Murphy are a few who graduated from Festival amateurs to Equity. Many actors we've come to love now perform in theaters across the country as well as on the screen.

Richard Hay grew from his training at Stanford University to become the renowned set and theater designer, whose reputation stretches across our country. His professional expertise touches all the Festival theaters — Elizabethan, Bowmer, Black Swan, and The New Theater (recently renamed The Thomas Theater).

Mr. Bowmer and Jerry Turner (a former Artistic Director of OSF) have both passed on, and new hands hold the reins, but excellent theater continues.

Ashland Today

What is Ashland like today? Let's start by exploring the streets of downtown Ashland. There are several art galleries, tidy shops and boutiques, small restaurants, including a Starbucks, a Christian Science Reading Room, a florist, a few banks, a few realtors, and a movie theater — the sorts of businesses you find in most cities, but here the businesses are perhaps smaller and the people more friendly. Most of the restaurants are used to the theater crowd and provide quick service.

The Plaza — at the foot of E. Main Street — has many distinctions: a fountain with Lithia Mineral Water, some specialty shops including a clothing store for children, a book store also for children, and a shop that sells international clothing and jewelry. You will also find a storefront office inviting you to river raft.

January 1, 1997 a huge, warm rainstorm hit Southern Oregon, melting snow, resulting in severe flooding in the Plaza area. Three feet of rushing water inundated the shops and the merchandise, especially clothing, as well as creating havoc with the bridge. Clean-up following the storm was a huge task. The flooding knocked out Ashland's water supply for a few weeks, so the only working Laundromat was fed by an artesian well. What to do with all the soggy and muddy clothing? Family friends (owners of Small Change, a children's clothing store on the Plaza) recently filled me in on some of the details.

A friend of theirs in Medford knew the owner of a Medford Laundromat. The friend gathered about 20 of her friends and rented the Laundromat after normal hours. Taking truckloads of those soggy clothes, they had a laundry party into the wee hours of the night.

These helpers returned the now clean clothes to Ashland the next day (which was sunny) and hung them on racks set up in the owner's driveway up in the hills. After ironing the merchandise, my friend had a big "Flood Sale" to move out these clothes — store space for this sale being provided by a nearby business not affected by the flooding. Hearing of the sale, towns-people happily bought these clothes, but some insisted on paying the full price. They didn't want to benefit themselves at her expense.

Meantime, since there was still no water, a communal port-a-potty was set up on the driveway. The local news-crew came out to check up on the doings, especially the port-a-potty, which had been adorned with Christmas lights, magazines, and a guest register. Both the potty and the owner made the evening news. Ashland folks are good neighbors with a sense of humor!

Damage to structures and the bridge was extensive. The buildings were upgraded, enhancing their beauty; but the bridge was removed, the channel straightened and widened, before a new bridge was installed. The bridge between Lithia and The Plaza is therefore quite new.

Outside the Plaza area — Strolling E. Main Street you find a variety of shops, restaurants, and art galleries. (Among these shops are a few that have had resident cats.) Those having had cats are Tree House (the children's bookstore on the plaza), Lithia Shoe Store (232 E. Main

Street), and Bloomsbury Books (290 E. Main). Before his passing, it was fairly common to see the Bloomsbury Books cat, Orlando, sleeping among the books displayed in the front window. The shoe store cat also passed on and has been replaced by a friendly yellow tabby, and his owner requests that customers "Please keep the door closed!"

Outside the downtown area there are a few small shopping malls. Here you find services such as Laundromats, a large movie house, a Radio Shack, and many other small businesses.

One unique program the city has offered is a plaque dedicated annually to that year's "Tree of the Year." They're still offering this plaque and I know where two of these special trees are. (You can find a list on-line.) The first plaque was offered in the late 1980's for a large, then nearly perfect Cypress tree on Briscoe Elementary School property at the corner of North Main and Laurel. Either lightning or disease badly damaged the tree, and it was severely pruned. Arborists are taking loving care of it, and it's beginning to fill out to its former beauty. The second tree I've located is in Lithia Park. See if you can find it.

Southern Oregon University

Ashland main streets (E. Main and Siskiyou) join beyond the downtown area. At this intersection are the new fire station and the rebuilt City Library. The library welcomes out-of-towners, allowing you to acquire and use a library card to check out books, etc. Continuing down Siskiyou a short distance you come to Southern Oregon University, a four-year liberal arts school. (Both the Theater and Music Departments have a strong connection with the Festival; you'll find some of the same names on the staffs of both organizations.)

The new campus Library is a beautiful, imposing structure, and its good collection of books and services are shared with visitors other than students — such as townspeople and tourists — like the Ashland City Library mentioned above. (Strolling through the campus one afternoon, we happened across a well-known actress from the Festival. We were looking for a particular building, and we must have looked like the famous puzzled tourists because she asked if she could be of help. She graciously answered a few questions and then invited us to use the library — which she clearly admired.)

On a small hill on campus overlooking Siskiyou is their new small but interesting museum with its changing exhibits. Ashland Public Schools bring classes here on field trips. The museum has much material for which there's really no place to permanently exhibit, so the frequently changing displays give the public a chance to get a look at some of it. If you have visited once, go back again and see something entirely "new."

The University is also in the process of acquiring a unique and large collection of historic and valuable musical instruments from local Jack Schuman. Parts of the collection have been displayed, and more will be as there is space to do so. Presently they are available to Festival musicians to borrow and use in performances.

If you take a walk through the campus, you'll find there are several other interesting places — some having sculptures, singly and in groups. These sculptures are mostly not of famous people, but artistic, freeform shapes. Since it's a fairly small campus, stroll around and find them. The bookstore, located in a student union building, contains the usual selection of materials and textbooks, and various sportswear with the school logo on it. If you're a collector of clothing with university logos or if the weather turned out to be cooler than you expected, here's where you can make a purchase. If you know a youth who is interested in attending SOU and you're curious about course offerings or other information, this would be your source for answers.

Also on campus is a lap pool, which non-students can make arrangements to use. (Again, the bookstore would be a source of information.)

Since this establishment is open year around with convenient hours and location, it's a handy place to know. To make contact if you need answers but prefer not to explore on foot, check the Ashland phonebook under Southern Oregon University Athletics and Recreation.

Returning to the downtown area, at the Information Center you can sign up to take a bird walk or a walking tour through the downtown area to see some of the historical buildings — ones you've passed for years without really seeing them, like the Ganlard Opera House up on the second floor.

When you return to the plaza, walk to the end of the block and there is Lithia Park, which we'll soon explore.

(Just to get oriented, if you have a car, drive north on Main Street. After crossing Lithia Creek you soon find Main Street has become old Highway 99, and in a few miles you come to the small towns of Talent and Phoenix before arriving at south Medford. Here you'll see the turn-off to Jacksonville — discussed in a separate chapter.)

The Festival

The Festival has things to do other than attending the plays.

Check with the box office or the glassed-in bulletin board across the street from the box office for listings of special events. There might be lectures or concerts in Carpenter Hall, lunch lectures in Lithia Park, or back-stage tours. Some of these events require purchased tickets while others are first come, first served.

Back-Stage Tours – These tours, offered daily except Monday, are popular, so don't fail to get your tickets from the box office, a day in advance if possible. (There is a fee.) Even if you've taken the tour before, each visit you have a different guide resulting in each tour being unique; so by all means, go again. On the day of your tour some member of the production company will guide you in small groups. It could be an actor you saw perform the night before, or it could be one of the knowledgeable technical people. Your guide will be able to answer questions about the staging, lights, sound, or special effects. "How do they make it sound like a storm?" "How do the fight scenes seem so real without injuring the actors?" It's a chance to get answers to your burning questions.

You'll see computers and may be surprised at the part computer technology plays in creating the illusion of the plays. The tour may take you to the costume shop where you can see how the costumes, armor, and wigs are constructed. And the tour may direct you to the Festival Welcome Center, where there are interesting pictures that help you learn Festival history and also costumes (from past productions) mounted on mannequins.

The tours take about two hours.

Carpenter Hall –The Christian Science church which once occupied this venue has moved to a different location, and the Festival bought the old church and uses it for lectures and concerts. These programs usually start around 12 noon. Tickets are available in the Festival box office. (The perimeter mirrors rightly suggest it's sometimes used as a dance studio.)

The lectures usually share insights into the plays and/or their historic periods, and are conducted by actors and directors from the company or by visiting scholars. There is customarily an opportunity to ask questions.

The concerts have featured Festival musicians or dancers. Every year the offerings differ, but these concerts have given these performers a chance to do something entirely different than you see in the scheduled plays. One year the dancers did tap, for instance. Or the concerts may give these talented people an opportunity to further explore period music or dance, or 20th century works, or even explore some compositions composed by the musicians. Also the music provides an opportunity to see different instruments — period pieces — you don't see in the plays. Local Jack Schuman has a remarkable collection of instruments, mostly period, that have been featured in some of these events. (These instruments, by the way, are now housed at Southern Oregon University, just down the street from the Festival.)

Talks in the Park – These are informal sessions with actors, directors, or designers — from inside the Festival or visiting scholars — and other festival personnel. You're invited to bring a lunch and sit on a bench adjacent to the theater and listen to these professionals reminisce or inform you and answer your questions. These talks also start at 12 noon, last about 45 minutes, and are free.

There are two ways to get to this venue, the Bill Patten Garden, which is just below and beyond the Elizabethan Theater. A path to the left and beyond the theater leads right to it. The other way is to enter Lithia Park from the Plaza and aim for the path immediately to the left leading up the hill. Once at the top you'll recognize it by the permanently mounted wooden benches.

Other Free Festival Offerings – One of these is the post-matinee discussion, where an actor in the matinee production joins the waiting fans after the show for an informal interview and question and answer session. You can also enjoy watching set change-over. Bring your lunch or a cup of coffee and watch the techies change from last night's set to the one you'll see tonight. Their work is so carefully choreographed! (Both are in the Allen Pavilion.)

Tudor Guild Gift Shop – "Gift Shop" is perhaps not the perfect term for this lovely shop.

You can buy the Festival Publications: *The Annual Souvenir Program* (which includes pictures and bios of the actors, directors, designers, etc. for the year) *Prologue,* and *Illuminations* (both of which discuss different aspects of the plays), plus the annual Festival T-shirts, scripts and other theater-related books, cookbooks, and travel books (particularly for England, Scotland, Wales, and Ireland). You can purchase CD's by Festival actors and musicians. Also DVD's and CD's of music and Shakespeare plays recorded by professionals independently of the Festival are for sale. There's a small but nice collection of children's books. Jewelry, masks, and mugs are also available. So are various yummy candies and cookies. That's not the whole inventory, but it gives you a hint of the pleasures to be found.

Green Show – Before the evening performances — weather permitting — there is a "Green Show" on the broad low stage on the bricks in front of Bowmer Theatre. (I say weather permitting, referring not only to the possibility of rain but also hot temperature. If the thermometer reads above a certain level dancers, for instance, may not perform.) By way of history, for years you could see professional dancers perform mostly modern dance accompanied by the Terra Nova Consort. The dancers had their roots in New York, while the Consort started as Festival musicians. They have become a very proficient ensemble, playing historical, folk, regional, Gershwin — you name it — on a variety of modern and historical instruments. The dancers are gone, but the musicians still perform a few nights each season.

The Green Show has changed directions. It's now a mix of music, dance, and humor, with some acts more successful than others, but all give performers not otherwise connected with the Festival a chance to showcase their work before a live audience. You never know how the Green Show will pan out or what it will include, but the intent is to entertain you and get you into the mood to see a play. These short performances are free and start around 6:45 p.m. A word to the wise: If you plan to sit on the grass, bring something plastic to sit on, because they water the lawn!

Here are Some Places Near the Festival that You'll Want to Visit

Lithia Park

Lithia Park is 100 acres of beauty in the hills above Ashland and adjacent to the Festival grounds. Getting to the park is very easy. The Festival box office faces on Pioneer Street. Follow this street past the Elizabethan theater, and within a block you're immediately in the park. This street soon becomes a two-way dirt road, which gently winds among the native trees and then dips down to cross Lithia Creek. On the other side of the creek you can turn either to the left and explore other dirt roads in the wild area above the park, or you can turn to the right and discover the landscaped Lithia before the road returns you to the plaza. (The other way into the park would be to start with the plaza, walk away from E. Main to the end of the block, and the park lies before you. This entrance to the park is available year-round with no mud puddles.)

This is a fairly large park, and part of it might be better explored on a bike or in a car. Recently while driving in the Lithia hills we came across a barricade, which prevented us from driving very far on this dirt road. I don't know if this is permanent. Joggers frequent these dirt roads. We've recognized several festival performers working up a sweat here. The roads that loop through the upper regions are also popular with bikers, and there's an occasional bike race. Drive cautiously.

John McLaren designed the park, located on the site of Old Ashland Mill, in early 1900's.

He is also the Scot who designed San Francisco's famed Golden Gate Park. Both parks have areas of untouched wilderness next to areas of manicured lawns, majestic shade trees, mature shrubs, well-tended flowerbeds of bright annuals, a Japanese garden, and a rose garden. There are occasional fountains, sculptures, and monuments, most built and dedicated to the memory of some-one who has done much good for the city. There's also a grove of precisely spaced sycamore trees.

The sweeping lawns are divided into smaller areas on different levels and separated by barriers of trees and shrubs. If you want to settle down to snooze, read a book, or indulge in the popular pastime of "people-watching," there are benches and wide expanses of tailored lawns. We even saw a group of people playing croquet. (They had provided their own wickets and equipment.)

A trail leads to a gazebo providing shelter from the sun or inclement weather and also has drinking fountains with both mineral and non-mineral water. Mineral water is an acquired taste, and here you can sample it, an experience not to be missed, though perhaps not frequently repeated. It is an act of kindness that the park also provides nearby drinking water of the "more usual" taste.

Some paths lead to Lithia Creek, which flows year-round through the length of the park. Occasional steps lead down to water level with shady places to sit and read or chat. In the landscaped area, the creek makes a series of three- to four-foot drops over concrete slabs or rocks and is popular with waders, though authorities frown upon this activity. Several footbridges cross the stream, allowing for easy access from the parking along the street.

Lithia also has a children's playground, a volleyball court, tennis courts, a swimming hole, and many paved paths for strolling. Benches overlook two ponds, which have provided homes for ducks and graceful swans, but there's been talk of removing the swans because people, particularly children, love to feed them people food (which is unhealthy for the birds) and because the swans are more beautiful then well behaved. (During a recent visit, we saw no swans, so apparently they're now gone.)

Picnic tables dot the space between the wild and the landscaped areas. Be aware that some years the conditions are popular with yellow jackets, which compete with you for your lunch.

Public restrooms and drinking fountains are available. These drinking fountains can be found in and near the park, notably on the plaza and under the gazebo in the park.

We've visited the park many times, often on weekends, and found it crowded not just with tourists but local families. Parking slots are scarce near the popular children's area where papas (more often than mamas when we were there) swing their toddlers, and older children climb over the slide structure.

Going back to the plaza entrance to the park, and just inside the park, has been a white statue of Abraham Lincoln. Vandals have been fond of absconding with the head, so occasionally Lincoln is headless while a replacement is formed. On our last visit the statue, though not its foundation, was gone, perhaps for repairs. Just beyond this statue, a footpath climbs the hill to the Bill Patten Garden, a flat area with benches, used by the Festival for the noontime Talks in the Park. (There's more about these talks in the chapter about the Festival. pp. 35.) In front and just below the bench area is where you can find Brass Rubbing. There are several pieces of tactile art under the supervision of volunteers who will show you how to do this artistic activity.

Guided nature walks through Lithia are provided, usually Sunday or Wednesday mornings. Check with the Information Center adjacent to the Festival on E. Main Street about the times of these free nature walks. Weather permitting, you stroll the easy trail for about an hour. Wearing comfy shoes is about the only requirement. The walks start at the feet of Lincoln's statue.

An interesting phenomenon that we've noticed: on very hot days when you step into the park there is a noticeably cooler feeling. Visiting Lithia on a hot afternoon is a comforting experience!

In summary, Lithia Park is a popular, well used, lovely setting for a variety of activities. Each area has places to sit and enjoy the beauty. The rose garden has paths so you can wander through and smell the fragrances, and the Japanese garden also has paths to explore. This park is inviting and easy to get to. Be like a local and spend time here to unwind.

Rare Events

The Band Shell

There have been two main types of presentations here in the shell — ballet and concerts. Largely for financial reasons these activities have not always been presented, but if you're interested, check out the possibility that they'll be on again.

How to get there: Start at the plaza, the foot of Main. Follow the road that hugs the park — Winburn. The children's play area is at Nutley Street, and the shell is just beyond the play area, so if you're driving, park anywhere near there. Since the presentations in the shell are popular, allow time to find a parking place. If your motel is near enough, walk to the shell and save the possible frustration of competing for parking places.

Ballet in the Park

In past years a ballet performance has been offered by Ballet Rogue, a valley company, Monday evenings at 7:30. Perhaps they'll do it again this summer.

A few years ago we saw the production of *Hansel and Gretel*, choreographed by their Artistic Director. Stage lighting was used, but the performance was short, getting out about 9:00 p.m., so it wasn't quite dark and the audience wasn't sitting in the dark. The first few rows of seating were moveable wooden benches, behind which a few people sat in camping chairs they had thought to bring. But most of the audience sat on blankets, etc., on the gently sloping grass. It was a large, attentive audience — ranging from infants to senior citizens — appreciative of the young talent.

These performances were free — no tickets, no passing the hat. But it costs to produce these programs, and on the night we were there the company manager did make a reasonable pitch for financial support, which apparently offended nobody.

These ballet productions haven't been presented the last few years, but they were popular and may return.

Concerts in the Park

My last information indicates that in 2011 there were a few concerts, but after that it's anyone's guess. We have never attended one of these concerts, but we've heard them from a distance. If concerts are to be held, they're announced on the shell's bulletin board. During the summer months they have been on Thursday evenings — again free to the public.

Horse-Drawn Rides

Horse-drawn carriage rides have sometimes been offered through Lithia and surrounding area, mornings into early afternoon, and sometimes early evenings. The rides when available started at the plaza, and the driver told you prices and specific times. He was also happy to tell you how you could rent him and his rig for other routes of your choice. As with other independent contractors this fun service may or may not be offered this year. It was in 2012. Look for it.

Ashland Market

This market is not strictly speaking a part of Lithia Park, but it's right across the street and feels like an extension of the park.

If you've ever attended an arts fair, you'll have an idea of what the Ashland Market is like. On the several occasions we visited, we found artisan's booths showing lovely jewelry, tie-dyed clothing, hats, pottery, bird feeders, wind chimes, furry slippers, photographs, paintings, etc. — wonderful crafty items invitingly displayed in a unique and lovely setting. One enterprising woman was offering basket-making lessons to enthusiastic patrons, baskets made from dried seaweed ropes and decorated with other types of seaweed. Every year is a little different, so you may not find all of these artisans when you visit.

The market has been in two locations. This again is occasionally subject to change each year.

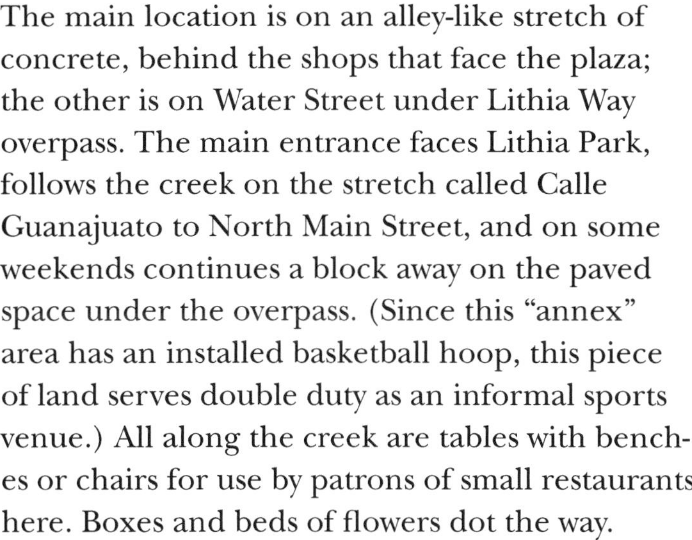

The main location is on an alley-like stretch of concrete, behind the shops that face the plaza; the other is on Water Street under Lithia Way overpass. The main entrance faces Lithia Park, follows the creek on the stretch called Calle Guanajuato to North Main Street, and on some weekends continues a block away on the paved space under the overpass. (Since this "annex" area has an installed basketball hoop, this piece of land serves double duty as an informal sports venue.) All along the creek are tables with benches or chairs for use by patrons of small restaurants here. Boxes and beds of flowers dot the way.

Located at the main entrance we have seen an easel listing times and names of that day's live entertainers — small informal musical groups, usually — who perform at a central, cleared area. Once when we were there, a mime strolled among the booths, entertaining as he went. Remember, though, that this is a live area, subject to change.

In any event, this market is interesting, located in a charming, shady setting, and the vendors are relaxed and friendly.

There have also been farmers markets on some weekdays. Check with the Information Center for times and locations — both in Ashland and Medford.

What Can I Do that Doesn't Need a Car?

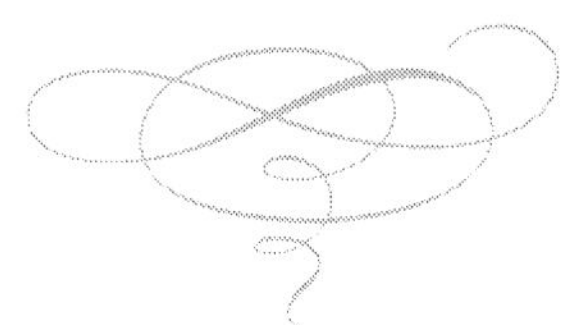

Since there is no way to know where each of you would be staying, as far as this book is concerned, everything starts from Ashland — often, specifically, the location of the Festival, at the corner of E. Main and Pioneer. (When the Information Center is mentioned, that frequently refers to the Chamber of Commerce booth next door to the Festival's Black Swan Theater on E. Main near Pioneer. For exploring areas outside Ashland, you should have a map showing the highway numbers.)

But first, what's there to do within walking distance of the Festival?

Lithia Park

One pleasant thing to do, particularly on a warm afternoon, is to take a stroll through the park. It's a large park with many places of interest, and is described in the chapter on *Lithia Park* (pp. 42).

Festival Doings

There are many things to do at the Festival, and they, too, are discussed in a chapter of their own (pp. 35). Be sure to allow time to do all or most of these. They're enriching.

Shopping

If you want big box stores, you'll need to go to Medford. But Ashland provides a large number of charming small stores and boutiques, some of which have been there many years, speaking for their customer satisfaction.

This book isn't serving as a directory of local shops, but a few are worth mentioning. Exploring the Plaza itself you find shops offering such items as gifts, children's books, international wares, and clothing — Small Change for children and Inti-Imports for adults. Around the corner from the plaza going north is a new store featuring Native American items. Walking down Main Street in the opposite direction, you'll find other clothing stores and shoe shops. There's a travel shop, which offers not only clothing but also other travel-related merchandise. Also along the way you'll find jewelry and bead shops plus an amazing hat shop. If you like shopping, have fun exploring.

A few blocks from the Festival is a very helpful shop, the **Northwest Nature Shop** at 154 Oak Street. Oak is one block north and parallel to Pioneer Street, the street where the Festival is located. Here you can find maps (different types of local, regional, and national maps), and guidebooks such as hiking and field guides (particularly about birds and plants in the area). In addition there's a mix of other books, some on local history and some providing details about regional wonders such as Crater Lake. They also sell things like birdhouses, bird feeders, samples of rocks and minerals, and wind chimes. We make an annual trip to see what's new. As the store's name suggests, the owners are interested in the

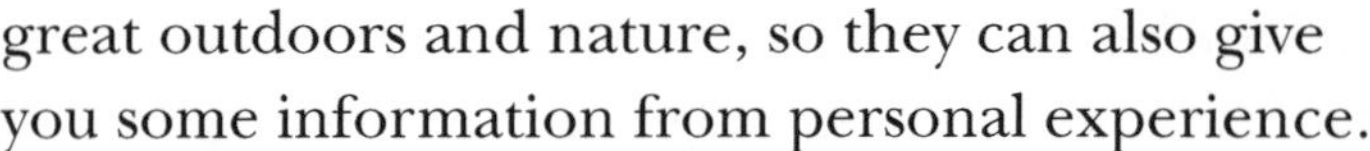

great outdoors and nature, so they can also give you some information from personal experience.

Ashland Market

I've mentioned this space elsewhere, (pp. 48) but if you've ever attended a street craft fair, you'll have an idea of what the Ashland Market is like. Every year is individual, so you might find different artisans and wares each time you visit.

This market's location is subject to change, also, but it's usually on the alley-like stretch of concrete behind the shops that face the plaza. The main entrance faces Lithia Park, follows the creek on a stretch called Calle Guanajuato to North Main Street, and on some weekends continues a block on the paved space under the overpass.

In any event, this market is interesting — even if you don't buy anything — located in a charming, shady setting, and the vendors are relaxed and friendly.

Farmers Markets

There have been farmers' markets on some weekdays rather than weekends. Check with the Information Center by the Festival for times and locations — both in Ashland and in Medford.

We found wonderful fresh fruits and vegetables plus sweet-smelling, tasty fresh-baked bread. Oh, yummy is the word! Unless food bores you, give it a try.

Restaurants

The blocks surrounding the Festival abound with places to eat. Most are small establishments where the service is usually excellent, because they cater to theater-goers. Restaurants are frequently changing, but as of this writing you can find Italian, French, Mexican, Indian, Thai, and a variety of other cuisines. You can find stores specializing in chocolates and ice cream. And don't miss the basement restaurant, Munchies, where you can get good hamburgers. (Munchies has been refurbished after being scoured out by that devastating flood.)

The Oregon Cabaret Theater, a combination restaurant and theater, is a former Baptist Church — and it's a small venue. The small stage accommodates only a few actors, so the cast members play multiple roles. But they tackle any musical that strikes their fancy and do it with fun and style. Before curtain time, a fine dinner is served from a small menu as a part of the evening's doings. Since the Cabaret's staff presents both the dinner and the theatrical production, you can be sure the dinner is served with dispatch. The ticket price does not include the price of your dinner. This is billed separately at your table at the time of serving. Reservations are a must.

The Oregon Cabaret Theater is located a block from the Festival at First and Hargadine streets (parallel to E. Main and the same street from which you enter the Festival/public parking garage). The plays are presented on different days depending on the time of year. Information about the current production — the title of the play plus days and hours of performance — are posted outside the theater. Or you can write for information (P.O. Box 1149, Ashland, OR, 97520) or find it on the web at www.oregoncabaret.com.

Walking Tours

There are historic and bird-watching tours available in the Festival area. You'll need to make reservations for these attractions at the Information Center. The walks are neither long nor arduous, but they are interesting and informative. The historic tour introduces you to those buildings you may have passed without realizing how interesting they are and their meaning to the community. As for the bird walks, if you're an avid bird watcher from out of the area, you may find a few surprises.

Books

There are several bookstores here. One shop — Tree House, on the Plaza — specializes in children's literature, and the owner is very knowledgeable and helpful. Another shop down E. Main Street offers a number of books dealing with Shakespeare. I don't know the name, but it's on the alley by the Varsity Movie Theater. A third, Bloomsbury Books, is a bit larger and offers a more eclectic stock. Also, the Festival's

Tudor Guild Gift Shop, has a large selection of books related to theater or historic periods, plus scripts of Shakespeare plays and those of other authors whose works are being offered during the festival season. (And of course, it sells much more, non-book merchandise.)

If you want to buy one of a few translations of the Bible, or just want to read and don't want to buy a book, you can visit the Christian Science Reading Room (near the movie theater). Here you can read *The Christian Science Monitor.* Another venue with no strings attached is the Ashland Public Library, further down E. Main Street, where it becomes Siskiyou, at the edge of the downtown area. Here visitors can acquire a library card and check out books — of course with the understanding that the books will be returned during your stay in town.

During the Holidays

If you're in town on July 4th or right after Thanksgiving when Christmas officially starts, you can join in these annual holiday celebrations. They include parades, etc. See the chapter on "Ashland and Holidays" (pp. 59).

Child Care

In past years, childcare provided by trained professionals has been available. Contact the Chamber of Commerce Information Center to see if it's available during your stay in Ashland.

From here on out, you'll need some sort of transportation — skates, a bike, public transportation, or a moped will do at first, but beyond that you should have a car or motorcycle. There are city parks, schools that allow the public to use their tennis courts, the golf course, the YMCA, the Scienceworks Museum, to name a few. Explore on your own or continue with me as I visit wonderful places in the nearby counties and Northern California.

Ashland and Holidays

Before moving on to other locations, let's consider how Ashland celebrates a few holidays — and they do have fun.

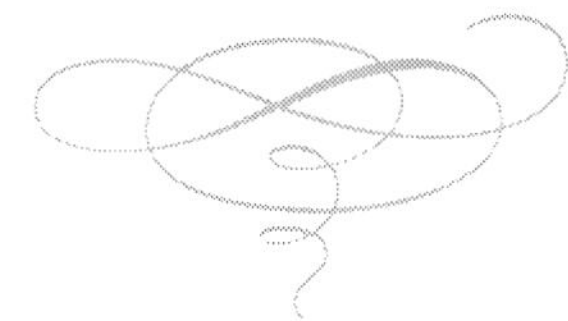

Fourth of July celebrations are a big deal in this town. They include a morning parade, a citywide picnic in Lithia Park, and various other activities all day. It was a July 4th celebration that marked the beginnings of what is now the Oregon Shakespeare Festival.

The parade, traveling down Siskiyou, includes patriotic and general floats and marching groups — including, of course, local school bands. As the parade winds down, the watchers stroll down to Lithia Park where there is an assortment of booths, many of which sell picnic-type food. From there, people assemble at the bandshell to hear more music and expect to hear — the highlight of this part of the day – a member of the Festival, orating. We heard Barry Kraft recite the Declaration of Independence, and he encouraged the audience to cheer or boo as if each person was reacting to ideas he was hearing for the first time. Some of the audience really got into it!

If you happen to be in Ashland on July 4 evening and don't have tickets to the Festival, get over to the Southern Oregon University athletic field before dark and find a place to watch fireworks. The location is at the intersection of Rt. 66 and Siskiyou as you approach I-5. If you can walk this distance or arrange to be dropped off you will be glad you did, for this is a popular event; and even with police directing traffic at numerous corners, the traffic jam afterwards can be almost as memorable as the fireworks.

Before the professional displays start, expect to see families of townsfolk gathered around on lawns of the college or the nearby public school, in front yards, and along the streets for their own amateur detonations of noisemakers, sparklers, and various small-scale pyrotechnics. The sound of the bang, bang, bang of firecrackers and the swish and booms of other eruptions will be accompanied by shrieks of excitement and the heavy smell of burning sulfur. It's a very festive time, probably about the same every year.

Typically the professional display starts with a series of loud non-visual explosions, reminiscent of the loud thumps on the stage heard before some Shakespeare productions, or the clearing of throat before a speaker starts orating for a restless crowd. Once they have your attention, the real fireworks begin. They're many and varied, and the appreciative audience will "ooh" and "ah" at the many colorful displays.

Having seen several public plaques honoring veterans of every former war and banners welcoming home recent military personnel, we shouldn't have been surprised at the amazing display of flag waving and joy. It's certainly different from the way people from big cities seem indifferent to patriotic things and instead concentrate on the color and noise of fireworks.

We got in on part of the celebrations one year and found it such fun, that we scheduled a free day on another year to take part in the whole

thing. It was indeed delightful, and we were glad we did it.

Christmas is also filled with happy events. Since December is not a time we visit Ashland, I can't speak from experience, but I understand that celebrations are varied and many. Jacksonville also has many Christmas traditions. If I were going to be in the area in December I certainly would plan to spend time in both communities to join the locals in their fun.

Things kick off in Ashland the day after Thanksgiving when the whole town lines the streets for another parade, this one to greet Santa as he arrives. Other events in December include caroling, concerts, various special theatrical presentations, a Gingerbread House contest, craft fairs, and the ceremony presenting the community Christmas tree. There's a Candlelight Tour of Homes, those abodes chosen for a combination of reasons — because they're among Ashland's finest, they're well decorated, or they're softly and safely lit with old-fashioned candles.

For more information, contact Ashland Chamber of Commerce, P.O. Box 1362, Ashland, OR 97520.

Oh yes, if there's been snow and you're a skier, Mount Ashland is only five miles away, so bring your skis.

Museums

Many small towns, as well as larger towns — have their own museums on a variety of subjects, most tending to encourage you to appreciate their early days, including relics from early Native American days, pioneers, gold miners, involvement in regional and national wars, etc.

Each collection's excellence varies to some extent on how much interest the local people have in maintaining their displays. But if you're a museum person, you'll always find something to learn and appreciate, even if your fingers occasionally itch for a feather duster!

Ashland Scienceworks Hands-on Museum

Directions: From downtown Ashland take E. Main Street toward I-5. (E. Main and Siskiyou divide at the main Ashland fire station, where you take the left of this "Y".) The museum is at 1500 E.Main near Walker Drive, adjacent to the US Fish and Wildlife Service Forensics Laboratory, and provides ample parking.

This museum is interesting to explorers of all ages, but especially to children and young teens. All comers are encouraged to push levers, sit on scales, experiment with magnets, view themselves through interesting mirrors, etc., and so plan enough time to try the various exhibits on display. The museum also provides short lectures that are worth your time. When we visited, the talk was aimed at young children on the subject of fire safety. A personable young man gave the talk with a good sense of humor, and the audience of wide-ranging ages all had a good time while learning something new. I've been assured that these talks keep changing, so you could feasibly visit once a month or so and see something different each time.

If you're traveling with kids who are getting a little bored with activities aimed at adults, give them a break and visit this visitor-friendly museum. It's fun for all ages.

As of this writing, hours are Wednesdays-Saturdays 10:00 a.m. to 5:00 p.m. and Sundays 12:00 p.m. to 5:00 p.m., June through August, closing an hour earlier the rest of the year. There is an admission fee.

They also offer summer day camps in week-long sessions. Nothing on their website indicated this is for local families, but you'll want to check with them at (541) 482-6767.

In my opinion, this is one of the best museums in the area. It's kept clean, and the exhibits frequently change. The staff is knowledgeable, well trained, and personable.

Across the parking lot is the **Wildlife Forensics Laboratory,** which is neither a museum nor a place of interest for the tourist. It is a place of business and is not open to the public.

Jacksonville

All of downtown Jacksonville is a historic area, so as a starter you can wander the streets in the downtown and pop into small stores that interest you. There may be a few homes you can visit that are in effect living museums. See the separate chapter on Jacksonville (pp. 73).

Gin Lin Trail

If you take a short drive out of Jacksonville on Hwy 238 you come to the **Gin Lin Trail.** (Check with the section on hiking in the chapter *Sports,* pp. 131, and you'll find more specific directions on how to get here.)

This is an outside museum, with a very short trail, which is pretty level and dirt surfaced. Here you can take a walk through a mining area, and learn about early methods of mining. There is evidence of hydraulic (water-powered) mining, for instance. This walk is free and self-guiding, though you should pay for the guide pamphlet (provided in boxes at the beginning of the trail) if you choose to keep the paper. Children would have no problem here, but a wheelchair probably couldn't make it.

Two Locations in Sunny Valley

Directions: Drive north on I-5 to Sunny Valley, about 15 miles from Grants Pass.

The Applegate Trail Interpretive Center is adjacent to the Grave Creek Covered Bridge (discussed in the chapter on *Covered Bridges,* pp. 217). The Wolf Creek Inn is across the highway a short distance. There are restrooms in both places.

The Applegate Trail Interpretive Center is a nicely put-together museum dealing with pre-statehood times of early Oregon. It shows information about the difficulties pioneers experienced traveling to Oregon and the impact the gold rush and railroads had on the area. Also there is information about the Indian wars and even some about nature: the geology, plus the flora and fauna of the region. Beginning the tour is a live chat followed by a filmed short talk by the man responsible for creating the museum; then you can wander at your leisure through the exhibits. A person in a wheelchair could enjoy this museum.

In front of the building, in the parking lot, are several covered wagons visitors can examine.

There is a fee for the museum.

Across I-5 and a few miles farther from Grants Pass is **Wolf Creek** and its historic inn where you can dine if the timing is right. The building has been restored and you can take a guided tour upon request. The tour takes you through some of the public rooms, which have been furnished in different periods representing the inn during various years of its history. If you prefer, you can wander through these rooms on a self-guided tour. The period pieces and displays are clean and attractive. After exploring the ground floor, you can climb the stairs and visit the ballroom and rooms used by guests to spend the night. Any room not rented may be entered and admired. Those rented out are closed to the public.

The Wolf Creek Inn was built in the 1880's to accommodate stagecoach customers on what was then Oregon Territorial Road. In front of the building is a pictorial display of its history.

Butte Falls

Directions: Take I-5 to Hwy 62 and turn toward Crater Lake. After 14 miles turn right on Butte Falls Road (north of Hwy 140). Butte Falls is mentioned on the turn-off sign and is about 16 miles from 62.

As mentioned in the chapter on *Rivers and Waterfalls*, (pp.179) there is a small railroad museum in this little town. It is mostly outside and is self-guiding.

Lake Creek

Directions: Take I-5 to Hwy 62 and turn toward Crater Lake. Then turn east on Hwy 140. Lake Creek is about 12 miles from Hwy 62.

Lake Creek is the home for Lost Creek Covered Bridge. Once off Hwy 140, you have to drive through the town to get to the bridge, so you'll notice that to say there are a dozen homes might be stretching it. But they do have a museum of sorts in their Community Hall, the large building on the left as you enter the town.

Our reason for coming to Lake Creek was to see the bridge. And we were glad we did. The bridge, used only by pedestrians, is the shortest of Oregon's covered bridges and looks rather fragile; but it's still standing, and we found it interesting.

Retracing our steps, we admired the dancing couple statue and then explored the Hall. The Community Hall had a lovely lady on duty to answer questions about the historical materials and pictures lining the wall. She's been around long enough that she could tell firsthand stories about many of the events in the pictures. There is a file of past issues of the local newsletter filling in information about past and present events.

We were utterly charmed by our hostess. I realize she won't always be the one on duty, but she made it all come alive. Perhaps the other hosts/hostesses are equally wonderful.

I'm so sorry this sweet place is enough off the beaten track that it won't see a lot of visitors, which is too bad.

Kerbyville Museum

Directions: Take I-5 to Grants Pass exit 55, then drive south on Hwy. 199 to Kerby.

On the way to Oregon Caves, the highway passes Kerby and the Kerbyville Museum. Since it has an unpretentious look about it, you may unknowingly pass it by. But there's a parking lot and some signs, so look for it.

This museum has a fascinating collection of historical displays, starting with Native American history and continuing through pioneer days, the gold rush, turn-of-the-century clothes, etc. Some manikins display everyday and special occasion wardrobes, including bridal finery. Two spaces are reserved for simulations: early telegraph equipment in an office setting, and a country store (including several items then for sale, such as food stuff — empty cartons I'm sure.) If you're a music buff look for the several pump organs placed here and there plus cases containing other instruments, particularly violins. If you're into military uniforms, they have a small room devoted to these items and related photographs.

When we visited, the curator had a lot to talk about and we finally had to nicely tell him we wanted to wander on our own, but he did share some interesting information along the way. When we were finished inside, he invited us to look at the outside display of forge and logging equipment, as I recall. One feature he was especially interested in was the authentic, very early log-cabin school. This is right in front where you park your car, though you may not recognize it for what it is. The timbers/logs are beginning to rot, so it's getting unsafe to enter this small building. As a result it's barricaded, but you can stand by the entrance and look inside. This spot is very historic, and there have been continuing steps to protect it.

There is a small fee. Display cases are close together, but I think a wheelchair could fit down the aisles.

We found so much to see here that we'd like to make a return visit.

Merlin
Pottsville

Directions: Take exit 66 from I-5, then follow the posted directions.

Most of the above museums are in a building, but this one is largely outside since a major part of its collection is big equipment — old (possibly historic) trucks and farming and logging implements. There are rows of different types of motor-driven or horse-drawn tractors, wagons, etc., which are arranged for the visitor's easy viewing. While wandering on your own is allowed, tours are also provided. Our tour, with a small number of people, was led by a knowledgeable member of the family running Pottsville. He shared stories and information and patiently answered questions.

In our group was a guy who had a farming background and had used similar tractors and other tools from his youth. Occasionally, after the guide's comments, he added his knowledge of how some piece was used, making our visit even more interesting.

In addition to this outdoors display, there are a few barns housing smaller items. Here frequent signs give some background of how an item was used or where it was found. One of the pieces displayed has to do with the aerial attack on Oregon during WWII.

Etcetera . . .

As mentioned before there are many museums in Southern Oregon. If you live for museums, while driving in the area when you see one, and you surely will, treat yourself to a visit.

Jacksonville

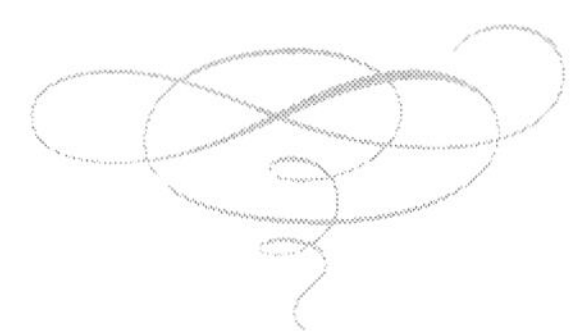

Directions: Take I-5 north toward Medford, and follow the signs to Jacksonville. This is about a 20-25 minute drive from Ashland.

Jacksonville is a historic city, deriving its status from its importance as a gold-mining town in the mid 1800's. Driving to Jacksonville on a paved two-lane country road, it's not hard to imagine what it was like to be here when there were horse-drawn wagons and dirt roads. Now Jacksonville is a quiet, charming burg with many buildings and shops dating back to its beginnings. These buildings are well preserved and both look and are authentic. The whole ambiance invites the visitor to stroll its streets, peeking into the many tourist-inspired boutiques.

The city of Jacksonville was founded in 1852, and the **downtown area** is a national Historic Landmark. Besides the inviting small shops and soda fountains (where you can get a sarsaparilla or soda), the visitor can find a few places dedicated to remembering its historic past. (In a controversial move, the contents of two museums were recently taken to Medford for storage, but there are efforts to return them. It's a rather sore spot with many Jacksonville citizens.) There are old churches and rectories — notably the **Presbyterian, Methodist, and Catholic churches** — all pre-1900. Also, typical of old towns, there's an **old cemetery** on the hill at the western end of town where the headstones tell sad stories of early pioneers and their children.

Exploring the historic past, you can take a walking tour of Jacksonville, following maps and brochures furnished by the Information Center at N. Oregon and C Street. One of the places listed in the downtown area is **Beekman Bank**, which has a small display focusing on banking in gold-rush times and remembering the day in 1915 when Mr. Beekman died. Admittance to the bank is not allowed, but there are large glass windows letting you see inside. Outside, beside the bank, look for the clear, transparent-covered display, which allows you to see below street level.

I'm going to mention two houses you used to be able to tour. Though they have been recently closed to the public, it's possible that they will reopen to visitors. Until then you can drive past them and at least remember their stories.

The first is banker **Beekman's house**, a few blocks away from the "shopping" area on South Stage Road, not far from the old Presbyterian Church. It's a nicely restored, yellow, two-story building. For years you could take a tour inside the building with the volunteer guides dressed in 1912 garb and discussing things only from that year. We visited on a day when there was a huge forest fire roaring out of control a few miles down I-5, with resulting heavy smoke. It was hard to not talk about it. The outside "greeter" allowed that some unusual things were happening, but inside the house everything was 1912. The servant in the kitchen was making muffins the old-fashioned way. When a visitor mentioned the possibility of an invention to make scraping the bowl easier — a spatula — she sweetly commented that such a tool would be very nice. Also, as a part of the tour, townspeople representing Mr. and Mrs. Beekman greeted us. They were costumed for the day and played their parts well. It was a pleasant visit, but for whatever reason (financial, maybe?) tours are no longer conducted. Perhaps they'll start again.

One part of this property that is still available to the public is a small **botanical garden** right next door, up the side street from the Beekman house. Local plants are labeled by name, so if you have a burning desire to know the name of a certain plant you just saw, you may find it here.

The second house tour I've taken, but has not been available the last few years, is the **Nunen house**. (There has recently been a bed and breakfast here with a restaurant in the carriage house.) The Nunen house was a prefab building, shipped by rail to this area where it was assembled. A more modern owner, when I visited, was a family that allowed tours to walk through their home and hear the history of the building. It meant that daily the family had to get up early and put all their personal belongings out of sight in order to give the house an early 1900's look. When they sold the house, the new owners didn't want tours going through their home. I understand that negotiations *may* have worked their magic, once again allowing tours of this lovely house. Ask at the Information Center.

One of the things that made this house memorable was that it came near to being destroyed by fire of unknown origin. The puzzling thing was that several houses of this design from the pre-fab company, located in many different areas in the U.S., had also been destroyed or damaged by fire. But why? Finally it was discovered that the handsome oval window over the staircase was acting like a magnifying glass and starting spontaneous combustion. (Remember way back when you were a kid, taking a magnifying glass and a piece of paper outside, focusing the sunlight on the paper, and watching the paper char before bursting into flame? Same thing.) When the cause was discovered, safety changes were made, and the building endures.

Leaving the historic area, today's modern Jacksonville has some niceties. A block off Main Street is a **city park**, popular with residents. Some picnic tables are under a cover, very welcome on hot summer days. A corner of this pretty spot is a concrete water park where laughing children play in the spraying fountains. It looks like fun!

Another big modern pleasure in Jacksonville is the famous **Britt Festival,** which offers concerts most summer evenings in their outdoor pavilion. The styles of music include jazz, classical, pop, blues, and country western; and the artists, performing as singles or in groups, are usually national celebrities. There is a fine concert orchestra (composed largely of local musicians) which performs alone or sometimes with nationally known soloists.

Seating arrangements vary. There is a small area of benches up front, but a larger, sloping area accommodates people with blankets for sitting on the ground. A few folks bring folding chairs. You can bring a picnic dinner or come early and eat in one of the city's fine restaurants — eating establishments that are used to patrons in a hurry to get to the pavilion before "curtain time." The Jacksonville Inn is our favorite.

Tickets are required, and since this is a popular event, reservations are very wise. Call (541) 773-6077 or (800) 882-7488 for theater reservations.

So much in this town has ties to its historic past, including this venue. The site for the Festival is the Britt Gardens, dating back to 1852 and belonging to photographer and horticulturist, Peter Britt. The grounds are pleasant to stroll, which is allowed in the mornings and early afternoons.

Jacksonville is a lovely place to spend quality leisure time. I've never seen anybody rushing, but I've encountered many smiling faces.

Medford

Directions: Take I-5 north to Medford.

The Medford area started as Rogue Indian land. Then, when gold was discovered in the Rogue Valley, Medford became a gold mining town. Eventually the soil was found to be fertile, and agriculture developed into what has become a huge enterprise. Soon after the town was incorporated in 1885 Medford became a stopover for the railroad, the beginnings of another large business. So, Medford has had many reasons for being important. The city is now the county seat of Jackson County.

Medford isn't the size or at the level of importance of Los Angeles, but it is the largest and most important city in Southern Oregon — for agriculture, manufacturing, lumbering, commerce, etc. Harry and David Country Store has its home base here, and you can take a tour of their factory and orchards. Many of the big box stores have branches here, most conveniently grouped together on State Highway 62. Also off Hwy 62, a short distance beyond Medford, is a fish hatchery that you can tour. Looking north or south on the horizon, there are mountains and mesas, especially Mt. McLoughlin and the Table Rock Mesas.

On the west side of I-5 is the older part of town and its business district. You can take self-guided walking tours to see some of the historic homes and businesses. The old movie theater has been remodeled into a beautiful, up-to-date theater house named for movie star Ginger Rogers, a resident of the area until her passing. Both movies and staged shows are presented here. In this building is also a mezzanine/art gallery displaying works largely by wonderful local artists.

To the individual who venerates shopping, perhaps one of the most interesting parts of Medford is its shopping opportunities. To mention a few, many of the big box stores such as Walmart and Costco are lined up on Hwy 62 — Crater Lake Hwy. On Biddle Road (the frontage road for I-5) is a Barnes and Noble. On the other side of I-5 (but in view of the highway) is a mall with more big stores. Many smaller, older shops are in the business district not far away.

In addition, Medford has many other businesses and industries, some of which offer tours. Also, it's the jumping off place for visiting so many area parks and forests. While we've made frequent shopping expeditions and drives past Medford on the way to someplace else, we haven't spent much leisure time in the city itself, aside from the below-listed tours. I know they have city public parks, one of which we've enjoyed for picnic lunches a few times. It's on Biddle Road at the south end of the shopping area, across the street from Sears. It has lovely shaded areas and easy access for wheelchairs.

The below-listed tours are presented in no particular order.

Business and Industrial Tours

Harry and David

Directions: In South Medford take Barnett Road (Exit #27) from I-5, turn to the left at Center Drive and aim for the Harry and David Country Store in the mall to the right. (There's a Tourist Information Center next door.)

Harry and David, brothers, started the famous mail-order company years ago, probably in the 1930s. It started with boxed pears and has evolved from there, shipping many fruits, candies, and other fine food gifts all over the world. They have also partnered up with Jackson and Perkins, one of the nation's leading producers, developers, and shippers of roses.

Tours of Harry and David are popular, and reservations are advisable. Tour arrangements can be made by phone, 877-322-8000 (the local number is 541-776-2277). On the tour, it's recommended that you wear comfortable shoes, for there's a bit of relaxed walking. Tours leave from the Country Store, and your visit passes areas where Jackson and Perkins roses and other plants are grown, pear trees produce their famous fruit, and chocolates are prepared and boxed. Tours are available Monday through Friday. Best days for tours are Monday through Thursday, because those are the most popular days, and when there aren't many visitors only a DVD is offered. According to a booking person, the very best time is Monday at 9:15 a.m.!

There is a fee, which, according to recent information, is redeemable for a coupon of the same value as the fee, which is applicable to purchases made at the store. And you may well wish to make purchases here. The fruit and vegetables look inviting, T-shirts are a good quality, and souvenirs beckon.

Tours have a way of developing and changing over the years. The tour I took started in a different location, and when waiting for our tour we strolled through the rose garden out front, finding our favorites and being impressed with the new colors that had been developed that year. Hopefully you can still do that by focusing on the location of the roses and returning after your tour for a leisurely stroll through the lovely plants.

Dogs for the Deaf

Dogs for the Deaf is in the northern Medford area at the foot of the Table Rocks, on 10175 Wheeler Road, Central Point.

Directions: Take I-5 to exit #30. Turn to the left to get to the other side of I-5 and look almost immediately for Table Rock Road. Turn to the right and follow Table Rock Road for perhaps 10 miles, until you get to Wheeler Road, where you turn to the left. You should see both the two large monoliths on the side of the mesa and also a sign on the left advertising an organization titled Dogs for the Deaf.

Another way to arrive at this point is to take Main north out of Ashland. This becomes Hwy 99, and once in Medford it becomes Riverside. Follow it to Table Rock Mountain Road toward the monoliths. You eventually see the sign on the left to Dogs for the Deaf.

Nestled at the foot of the Table Rocks, Dogs for the Deaf is an organization that trains dogs to help the deaf live independent lives. These dogs are also trained to help children and adults with physical, mental, or emotional needs. Most of the dogs are "rescue dogs" from shelters and are of a variety of breeds and sizes. The tour shows how the dogs are trained and behave in their new homes.

For more information see the chapter on Animals (pp. 115).

Railroad Historical Park

Directions: The beginning is the same as the above directions to Dogs for the Deaf. Once on Table Rock Road, before it crosses to the other side of the highway, immediately look for signs directing to Railroad Park. The address is 411 W. 8th Street. My maps show the park, but they don't call out 8th Street, perhaps because it's so small.

If you're fascinated by pre-diesel engine cars, you'll want to visit this railroad park. Once in the area, to get to the park you drive down a narrow road, almost an alley, past a fire station. The sign reads: Railroad Park — National

Historic Society Park. There are restrooms, a parking lot, and picnic tables.

The first thing you see is a green grassy plot with the picnic tables by the parking lot. Beyond that there are miniature locomotives and equipment built to 1-1.5 inch per foot scale. These replicas are faithful reproductions of full-size trains.

The park is quite small, but also there is a handful of full-sized railroad cars, cabooses, and an old steam engine you can climb on and over. There is also an operating telegraph system on site. The park is neatly cared for, making it look new. Hopefully, there are plans to expand it.

Also starting from this location, by the way, is the Bear Creek Green Way, a pretty path that winds under large trees and along the creek, designed for people to stroll or ride bicycles.

Cole Rivers Fish Hatchery (Lost Creek Lake)

Directions: Take I-5 north to Highway 62, following the signs to Crater Lake. Drive to the southwest end of Lost Creek Lake. (That's the near end as you come from Medford.) Turn to the left and follow signs to the hatchery.

On the highway to Crater Lake is Lost Creek Lake. Just before you see this large body of water, on the southwest corner of the lake, you will see signs that direct you to **Cole Rivers Fish Hatchery**, one of Oregon's largest hatcheries.

Lost Creek Reservoir dams Rogue River, which was once a very active spawning ground for trout and salmon. The dam destroyed those grounds, so the hatchery was built to produce the eggs and fingerlings of the fish very popular with fishermen. Arriving at the hatchery visitors can wander around the various concrete holding ponds, which are stocked according to the age and size of the fish — from just hatched to some about to be released to the local rivers and lakes. The species raised include salmon, steelhead, and rainbow trout. There's no charge for wandering.

There's also a **Visitor Center** adjacent to the ponds with restrooms and educational displays — exhibits regarding fish and local flora and fauna. There is also no fee to visit this part of the attraction.

A very short distance along this road (almost next door) is another visitor center, unrelated to the hatchery, right on the Rogue River, where you can sit on benches and enjoy the fast-moving stream. Either here or under the stately trees surrounding the building, is a pleasant place to enjoy a picnic. There are public restrooms. I'm not sure of the days the building is open, but since the area is not fenced, the tables and river can be enjoyed at any time. The restrooms are inside the building, so, obviously, they'd be available only when the building is open.

Butte Creek Mill

(Eagle Point, quite near Medford)

Directions: Highway 62 to Eagle Point. The address is 402 N. Royal Avenue. To get to the mill, drive .6 of a mile east on Linn Road; then turn left on N. Royal Avenue and drive about .3 miles.

The mill was built in 1872 and is the last mill west of the Mississippi that operates on water-power, grinding wheat to make flour. Visitors can watch the mill in action Monday-Saturday, (9-5) plus Sunday (11-5) with different hours for holidays. There's also a 16-minute instructional film. The whole visit takes about 30 minutes and is free.

There are also picnic tables on a grassy area behind the mill.

Other Venues

There have been other businesses and farms that once invited visitors to tour that no longer do so. Some of these venues have closed, and others simply discontinued tours. However, there might still be pamphlets out there that are out-of-date, advertising tours of these businesses. If you have one and a phone number is provided, call and see if you could still visit. They might welcome you. But do call in advance.

Small Towns

To those living in a big metropolitan area, like Portland or San Francisco, small town life might seem almost odd.

There's very little automobile traffic — ah, the stillness — or bicyclists, and public transportation is virtually unknown. Big billboards are for other people and places. High rises? What are they? (For years the tallest building in Southern Oregon was the Ashland Springs Hotel — nine stories high and the only building even approaching that height.)

One special thing about people who live in this simple environment is that many of them develop easy, friendly behavior to their neighbors and visitors. We have found pleasure in taking a simple picnic lunch and eating while sitting on a city bench — all the while enjoying the ambiance. Sometimes a local resident will join us, and we have lovely conversations. Alternatively, I've approached total strangers, asking about their area, and been greeted with kindness and openness to sharing what they know.

Most of these towns have a place of distinction — a bridge or a waterfall, for instance — that attracts visitors.

Here are a few small towns we've enjoyed.

Jacksonville

Directions: Take I-5 north to southern Medford where highway signs direct the driver to Jacksonville. Just follow the signs.

Jacksonville is one of the most famous and most interesting of small towns in Southern Oregon. The whole downtown area is a national treasure, and I devote a chapter to this lovely community (pp. 73).

Gold Hill

Directions: Follow I-5 north to exit #40.

Gold Hill is a lazy, quiet town. In fact, there was once a welcome sign reading, "A quiet town. All loud and unnecessary noise is prohibited." On a recent visit, we found this sign missing. Upon inquiry I found that the sign had originally been installed by the sheriff. Eventually some teenagers took it as a challenging trick. A few years later it turned up in a small town in Alaska, of all places. Go figure!

Gold Hill has a population of around 1,000 and is situated on the banks of the Rogue River. It traces its roots to gold rush days, the rich Gold Hill Lode being just northeast of the present town. In fact, there are still some gold-dredging activities in the area.

A few years ago we obtained a map of this historical town from the Gold Hill Chamber of Commerce, and with it we drove past homes and businesses related to its history. Also, there's a rather new Historical Museum with signs directing you to its doorstep, located in a residential area. It's well laid out and kept clean. There were three friendly local people staffing the displays on the day I visited in 2012.

People love to tell you stories about their areas, and one such story we heard was why Sardine

Creek on the edge of town, was so named. It seems that in prospecting days, a miner who was a loner would come to town to stock up on supplies. He rarely talked with anyone, but people noticed him. Since the only food they ever saw him buy was sardines, and the area he mined was up that little creek, they named it Sardine Creek.

Gold Hill has a Jackson County Library, which we visited. It's well equipped, especially considering the town's small size, and has a computerized check out/in system. The library shares a building with the City Hall and Chamber of Commerce. We found the librarians more helpful in telling about their town and area than the Chamber of Commerce on this particular afternoon.

There's an archery store in town, and an hour or more away (near Howard Prairie Lake Resort) we passed a resort-like area advertising archery activities. I don't know if this is a private club, but archery is an active sport in Southern Oregon, and here is a store that offers supplies and perhaps offers equipment for rent.

Rt. 234 is the highway dissecting Gold Hill, and Sardine Creek Road (on the north side of town) leads east into the wooded hills. About 4 ½ miles north of Rt. 234 is the **House of Mystery,** also called **The Oregon Vortex**. For a fee you can take a guided tour through the building and surrounding grounds that once housed an assay office for a gold mining company. The local Indians earlier called it The Forbidden Ground because of strange natural phenomena. The Guides do an entertaining job of displaying and explaining the phenomena.

Even if you think such places are hokey and you don't do hokey, certainly the countryside is beautiful, and the short drive out to the Vortex is lovely on that count alone. We visited on a hot day, and the shady drive was welcomingly cool and refreshing. Also, if you're looking for an easy way to entertain a youngster traveling with you, this would be a possibility.

Butte Falls

Directions: Take I-5 to Hwy 62, Crater Lake Highway. Turn right on to Hwy 62 and drive to just north of Rt. 234. Signs on the right direct to Butte Falls on Butte Falls Road, sometimes labeled Rt. 821.

The drive to this little town is through rolling farmland — very pleasant. Once in town we aimed for the city center, which has a square-block park. On one corner of the park is a statue surrounded by a chain-link fence. Who was it? Paul Bunyan's little brother, Ralph, of course, and I have no idea why he is so honored with this statue.

At another corner of the park is the library, once a diner in Medford, which was up for sale, bought, and moved to this location. Adjacent to the library is a railroad park housing a few retired engines, etc.

Butte Falls was once a booming logging town, with railroad connections to Medford. Logging trucks were developed, and eventually the train was no longer used. The town is not really a ghost town, but there's not a lot going on now. It's just a clean, lazy small town. It does have a botanical garden, Fairy Glen Botanical Garden, which I've never visited although it's just across the road from the falls. To get there one walks along the old railroad grade. There's also a fish hatchery somewhere nearby. Next visit, I intend to visit both attractions.

But our reason for driving to this small town on this day was to enjoy their falls, wide and low. For more information about our visit see the chapter titled *Rivers and Water Falls*, (pp. 179).

Lake Creek

Directions: Take Hwy 62 to Hwy 140, turn east, and drive about 15 miles to the turn-off. The road from Hwy 140 is a bit curvy and has a gravel surface, but you're only on it a short time.

This tiny dot on the road is the home of the state's shortest covered bridge, Lost Creek. While old, it's still standing, and pedestrians are allowed to walk on it.

Also, next door to the bridge is a small memorial park, which has picnic tables and a small stage that is used for special events. The atmosphere was surprisingly restful. The park is attractively landscaped with a manicured lawn surrounded by colorful plants and shrubs. Public restrooms are provided.

(Across the road a very loud cow mooed to us the whole time we were there. Since it was about noon I don't think it was milking time. But we certainly had her attention! May you be so lucky.)

After enjoying the park, we returned to the Community Hall and were enchanted with the friendly people in this very small town, right in the middle of cattle country. Their community center housed a small, interesting historical display, with a hostess to answer our questions

Next to the hall is a grassy area with a charming rotating statue of a couple dancing. We found that the dancers were not replicas of townspeople and had no connection with the town. The owner saw the statue in another part of the world, liked and bought it, and then installed it here. Why she chose this spot I don't know, but it's delightful.

Everything looked recently manicured and painted. There was a fire house, a post office, and a country store, but we saw no restaurants. Probably you could buy a few picnic supplies at the country store.

There are details of our visit in the chapters titled *Museums* (pp. 63) and *Covered Bridges*, (pp. 219).

Eagle Point

Directions: Take I-5 to Hwy 62, Crater Lake Highway. Proceed to Hwy 140, the exit for Eagle

Point. You're now on Linn Road. Drive about ½ mile and turn left. In a short distance you see a covered bridge — and a mill on the right.

My memory of the city itself is rather foggy. I honestly can't remember many details of this town except it looks very clean, is near Medford, and has two places of interest. The first is its lovely covered bridge — discussed in the chapter titled *Covered Bridges.*

The second is its "Butte Creek Mill," built in 1872 at 402 Royal North in Eagle Point. This is worth the trip in itself. It's a working bakery in a century-old water-powered grist mill and is open Monday-Saturday, 9:00 a.m. to 5:00 p.m. plus Sunday (11-5) with different hours for holidays. If you get there early enough, you can buy their most delicious blueberry muffins. Otherwise, they do sell other products, and after making a purchase, you can enjoy strolling through their historic building. After watching a 16-minute film you can watch the mill in action. Perhaps the best view of the exterior of the building is across the river in a small park, which provides picnic tables and a manicured lawn. This park is just around the corner after you cross the river.

Wimer

Directions: Wimer is reached by exiting I-5 at the city of Rogue River exit . Then drive past the rooster statue, jog to the left and find E. Evans Creek Road. Turn right. After about seven miles of driving through rural Southern Oregon, you arrive at Wimer. This burg is not shown on several of my maps, but trust me, it exists.

The most interesting thing about Wimer is its new covered bridge. There is more information about the bridge and the city in the chapter titled *Covered Bridges,* (pp. 217). Locals love their bridge and worked hard to get it replaced after it collapsed a few years ago.

They also like to engage the visitor in chatting about their bridge and "City Hall," a short block from the bridge. I got some interesting and unverifiable stories about the city hall, a Quonset hut with the words City Hall painted on the roof.

Merlin

Directions: Take I-5 to exit 61, Merlin.

The "business district" of this small town is not particularly distinguished. It has the requisite stores to provide for the simple needs of its citizens, but more interestingly it has several venues of note.

First, this small town is the home of **Wildlife Images**, although the description in their pamphlet says the city is Grants Pass. Hey, that's several miles south, but whoever heard of Merlin other than being the name of a famous magician of long ago? But Grants Pass is far better known and a better guide to the visitor.

Just follow the route suggested (in the chapter titled *Animals,* pp. 115) through Merlin and you'll arrive at this wonderful place that cares for injured wild animals before releasing them back into the wild. (The few that are injured in such a way that they can no longer care for themselves adequately, live out their lives here under the loving attention of the staff, volunteer and paid.)

Also located in this town is **Pottsville**, a largely outdoors display of farm and logging equipment, most of it being old enough to qualify as historic. There is also an inside exhibit of smaller items, most of which are not related to farming. Details of our visit are in the chapter *Museums,* (pp. 63). There is a fee.

Also in town, I've been told, there is a **"gay-nineties" theater**. I haven't seen it, but it's on my list of things to explore.

We also discovered that Merlin has a few boat landings for **rafting trips**. They list several possibilities of types of trips, their durations, and times of year. Its location is a few miles further from Ashland than Rogue River or Grants Pass, but not out of reason if you want to test their dock and fleet of "rafts."

Grants Pass

Directions: The most direct way to get there is to take I-5 north to Grants Pass.

Grants Pass isn't really a small town, but it is smaller than Medford and deserves mention someplace, so here it is.

A favorite place for us to visit is Wildlife Images, listed as being in Grants Pass, but is actually 12 miles north in Merlin. Be that as it may, leaving Wildlife Images there are two routes to get back to I-5 and then on to your next destination. Recently we elected to go south on back roads to Grants Pass. This meant instead of turning to the left as we exited the "Images" parking lot, we turned to the right and followed the gentle, rolling hills of Upper River Road. We continued to follow the rather small directional signs into Grants Pass, where Upper River Road becomes "G" Street and found ourselves in Old Town (Historic) Grants Pass. G Street (near 6th Street) is the main road here. The old town is largely shops in old, well-kept buildings. There are, among other types of stores, gift shops, antique stores, a wonderful shoe store, and a candy store with very yummy goodies and a friendly staff. We enjoyed strolling down G Street, entering shops that interested us, and of course Sandi's Candy Store was one of them.

There are several parks along the Rogue River – just blocks away from Old Town. Our favorite is The Riverside Park with its trimmed lawns and stately trees. To get there turn right on 6th from G Street and cross the river. Included in this park are a covered gazebo and a nice children's area with swings, climbing apparatus, and slides. Since there are many big trees, there's a lot of shade, which is very welcome in summer time. A picnic area and restrooms are provided.

There are many ducks and geese making the park their headquarters. Because of their large numbers, we found these birds borderline annoying but always amusing. The Rogue River is along one side of the park, and some of the birds practiced water landings and takeoffs. This area by the river is so inviting that we don't go to the picnic tables, but sit in our van (doors open) and enjoy the view and the ambiance.

By the way, across the river is a dock used by one of the companies that offer river cruises and rafting excursions.

When we were ready to return to Ashland, we took the exit from the park — the opposite side of the park from 6th Street, the entrance — and followed 7th Street to I-5. Shoppers beware, because you pass by a few blocks of famous big-box stores on the way.

Turn south to Medford and on to Ashland.

Drives

Southern Oregon and Northern California are rich with beauty, and one or more short drives will give you a chance to enjoy this lovely area. (When I say short, I mean wanderings that will take a few hours, rather than a few days!)

I present three drives, arranged in order of the difficulty of driving, starting with the simplest — best road, least curves, and the degree of climb being considerations. But there are many other roads to explore, and you may find others that are just right for you. In any case, be informed about the roads you explore before you drive them.

I have a pamphlet that discusses **National Forest roads**, and here are some of the tips it includes: "Most National Forest roads in Oregon are low-standard, one-lane roads with turnouts for meeting oncoming traffic … Food, gas, and lodging are seldom available along National Forest roads … Encounters with logging trucks are likely, even on weekends … Driving rules used on State Highways apply to National Forest roads." The brochure suggests that you buy a map of the area and notes (as quoted above) that some of the roads are low-standard. "If you plan to drive these roads, plan to encounter rocks and boulders, road washouts, downed trees, and brush encroaching on the roadway. For safety, use a vehicle suitable for rough travel and carry extra equipment such as axe, shovel, gloves, and extra fuel." This is important information if you explore on your own, but the tips don't apply to the first two drives described below, which are on quite good roads.

Evans Creek Road

This is a loop starting in the City of Rogue River and ending in Medford. Take I-5 to Rogue River exit 48 and stay on the north (or east) side of the river. Go a block into town, past the rooster statue in the center of the road, to a stop sign. Turn to the left for one block and then turn to the right on E. Evans Creek Road. Go straight on this road for about seven miles, enjoying the rural atmosphere, until you get to the small town of Wimer. Staying on E. Evans Creek Road, turn to the right until you get to where this road appears to dead-end at a service station and general store. Get out and stretch your legs. The people working in this store have always been friendly when we've stopped here, and you might enjoy treating yourself to a soda or snack.

Looking around to the right of the store you'll see the brand new Wimer Covered Bridge. There is more about the bridge and town in other chapters — *Covered Bridges,* (pp. 217) and *Small Towns,* (pp. 89).

Evans Creek Road bends at the store, and if you keep on this road you'll be driving through a combination of rolling farm country, stately trees that offer lovely fall colors, and conifers, roughly following the creek. The road has two-lanes and gently curves. While not a high-speed drive, it's not heavily traveled, and a slow beautiful drive can be relaxing. Enjoy Evans Creek Road for about 14 miles. You'll eventually come to Sam's Valley Road and then Table Rock Road. Turn to the right in both cases and head back toward Medford. Mt. McLoughlin rises majestically on your left.

Soon you'll arrive at Tou Velle State Park. The road splits the park in two — the first part is to the right and provides the opportunity to launch your boat into the Rogue River. The boat ramp is at the end of the parking area. This part of the park has been landscaped in recent years and now has manicured lawns and flowerbeds. If you aren't interested in the boat ramp part of the park, stay on the highway a very short distance further, and you arrive at Tou Velle Park proper on your left. Here is a lovely, expansive park with spacious lawns, multiple picnic tables, and stately specimen trees – which provide welcome shade. These tables are arranged so that you could enjoy a meal with just a few people or have a large group party. The road winds through the park, and on most of the drive you can see the river. During a visit here you may wish to wade. The water is rather shallow, but rangers recommend careful supervision of youngsters. There is a day-use fee.

After exiting the park and continuing on Table Rock Road, you soon cross I-5. Turning to the left you'll see signs to I-5 and Ashland, finishing this drive. The round trip is about 52 miles. Local residents say this is a lovely drive any time of year, but spectacular in the fall as the leaves become brilliant.

In some ways this is a rather tame drive, but it gives you a chance to see what rural Southern Oregon is like. And because of its tameness, it's really easy to navigate.

Mountain Lakes Drive

There are several beautiful lakes near Ashland, and a lovely drive of about 120 miles round trip will pass by most of them. You can start at either end of the drive, but for this description we'll start in Ashland. Begin the drive by leaving town on State 66, crossing I-5 on the way toward Klamath Falls. About a mile from I-5, beyond the motels, is a road called Dead Indian Memorial Road. (Sometimes the word "dead" is omitted.) This is the beginning of the drive.

What does this drive include? The route covers a generally good, two-lane road, circling up into the hills. (I use the word "good" advisedly, recognizing that in driving, that word varies in its meaning according to the driving experience of the driver. My first driving experience was on curvy, mountain roads, so if it's smoothly paved and lacking hairpin turns, it's a good road.) This road, though narrow and generally not appropriate for high speed, winds through hilly pasture and forested lands and at times follows or crosses a small creek. There are no hairpin turns. During the spring there are wild flowers amid the volcanic outcroppings. After the road rises to offer wide vistas of the Ashland area, the road proceeds through forested lands and soon passes several lovely Alpine-like lakes before returning to Medford.

But let's back up to the start of this drive — just after crossing I-5. When you come to Dead Indian Memorial Road, go straight ahead on State 66 following the signs to **Emigrant Lake,** the first lake on this drive. (Please note Dead Indian Memorial Road, for we'll be returning to it after leaving Emigrant.) Emigrant is a Jackson County Park, and there's further information about the lake in the chapter on *Parks in Southern Oregon*, (pp. 149). This lake is a reservoir, and it's the one you see from I-5 as you arrive in Ashland from California. The amount of water in the lake depends on the amount of winter rainfall, so some years it looks bigger than others. Even with less water it's popular for fishing, swimming, rowing, boating, or just playing around. There's also a band shell at water's edge. Before entering the lake area — and there is a fee — there is a small store where you can buy simple foods. Fast foods are available inside the park, and there are picnic tables and restrooms.

Returning to State 66 go back to Dead Indian Memorial Road and turn right. Soon the road begins to rise into the mountains, winding through those forested lands, and there are a few places to pull off the road to view Ashland and the valley below.

Further along this road you'll find signs to several mountain lakes. The first one will be Hyatt Lake, then Howard Prairie Lake, then Lake of the Woods, and, finally, (after you've turned toward Medford on State 140) Fish Lake. All the lakes on this drive provide picnic tables and restrooms, plus boat ramps. Also, you can swim, boat, and fish in all of them. Except as noted, there are small stores where you can buy a snack or a cool drink. These stores also rent fishing equipment and make arrangements for small boat rentals if the urge to fish comes to you. The woods surrounding the lakes come down to water's edge and make quite lovely views. They also provide some cooling effect, especially welcome on a hot Ashland or Medford day. Plan a picnic or come for lunch or dinner in one of the restaurants.

Depending on the time of year and the amount of winter rain in the area, you will find varying amounts of water in these lakes, too. Hyatt and Fish lakes are reservoirs for Medford, and on a recent visit in late August, the water level was very low. But the woods surrounding the lakes and the lakes themselves were still lovely.

The first two lakes are Howard Prairie and Hyatt, about 17 miles from Ashland. Just before you reach the turnoff to the lakes, you come to a bend in the road that provides you with the first view of beautiful, snow-topped Mt. McLoughlin, an extinct volcano. Both lakes are popular for fishing and water sports, and both have resort/cabin and campground facilities. Because **Howard Prairie** is long and narrow, it has enough space for waterskiing, and in addition to offering a wharf, some houseboats, and sailboats, there's a marina, a restaurant and a Laundromat. Hyatt has some of the same amenities, though fewer and on a smaller scale. Both resorts at these lakes have restaurants. The hours vary, so call/look up on-line listings under the name of the lake for hours and days open. They're both quite beautiful lakes.

As you continue your drive, you go in and out of National Forests and past several bogs. There are some foot trails for hiking. Ranger stations can provide maps of the area, including information about the trails.

Nearing the next lake, **Lake of the Woods,** you see signs to "Resort and Rainbow Bay" which leads you to the lake. Unlike Howard Prairie and Hyatt, this is not a reservoir. It's a lovely spot, elevation about one-mile high, again with conifers down to the water's edge. The restaurant (Lake House Restaurant) — a rustic, nicely kept place — attracts Ashland people who come up occasionally for dinner. (Again check for hours and days open.) On the wall is a detailed map of the area, showing the trails that go up Mt. McLoughlin. There are roads to explore around the lake, some giving vistas of the lake and some of the mountain.

Returning to the main road and continuing about one mile, you come to State Highway 140, which is the start of the circle returning to the Medford area and then to Ashland. This road is wider and faster driving than the first road, though still beautiful.

Four Mile Lake and **Fish Lake** are both off State 140. About one mile after turning on to State 140 heading toward Medford you come to the turn off for **Four Mile Lake** on the right. The lake is listed as six miles in, and it is where the base trail that goes up Mt. McLoughlin begins. We recently revisited this lake and found that the beginning of the road had deteriorated a bit and was rather a washboard experience. We decided to try driving it for a while and found that the beginning of the road was the worst, and after persevering we easily made it to this beautiful lake.

Four Mile Lake is also a reservoir, and from the dam location we had lovely views of the back side of Mt. McLoughlin. In all, the area is peaceful and beautiful, inviting to the camper, fisherman, or hiker but less attractive for someone out for a few hours relaxation. There are other lakes with easier access for that.

Fish Lake is right by the highway near the Four Mile Lake turnoff and perhaps doesn't look as Alpine as the other lakes on this drive. But it's available for picnicking and camping, and hiking trails start here, though it has neither a store nor a restaurant. A fish cleaning station and a wharf are provided, and the speed limit on the lake is restricted to 10 miles an hour. Clearly, as the name suggests, this spot caters to fishermen. The elevation is 4,635 feet.

A short distance beyond Fish Lake is County Road 813 heading for the town of Butte Falls. Turn to the right on this road, and after about 12 miles you'll arrive at **Willow Lake**. It lies at the foot of the familiar side of Mt. McLoughlin, and the views are spectacular.

Willow Lake is the last in this series of lakes. So return to State 140, turn to the right, drive to Crater Lake Road (State 62) at Medford, and turn left. Then follow State 62 to I-5 and follow the signs to Ashland.

Although you could visit all of these lakes and stop to view their beauties in one day, you'd be rushing things if you really want to enjoy them. Swimming, picnicking, etc., would take more time. However, they're close enough to Ashland and Medford that you could enjoy one a day for a few days.

The Siskiyou Loop Drive

Remember the tips about driving in National Forest roads stated on the first page of this chapter? *Re-read them before embarking on this drive!* The Siskiyou Loop is shorter and better than those described, but it is a logging road and is the most challenging of these three drives. It's dirt and gravel, and it has its share of potholes plus some twists and curves, with no guardrails. However, it is an absolutely beautiful drive, rising high enough to get lovely vistas both of Southern Oregon and Northern California. For instance, there are places where you have unobstructed, clear views of Mt. Shasta. But don't try this road if you're uncomfortable with rough, mountain driving. On the other hand, if you're comfortable with the rough driving and have a car capable of the potholes, twists, etc. — high-clearance vehicles are recommended — give it a try.

If you'd like a map of this road, go to the ranger station in Ashland near I-5, on Washington Street, by the Arco Station. A brown sign indicates the place to turn. The rangers are very knowledgeable and full of information on the area. Ask for the map that shows The Siskiyou Loop.

We've found that the easiest way to start this drive is to go to Jacksonville and drive straight through town on State 238. Continue on State 238 until you reach the small town of Ruch where State 238 turns off. Don't turn, but stay on what now becomes Upper Applegate County Road, which passes Star Ranger Station and McKee Covered Bridge. (This bridge is an interesting place in and of itself, and it is discussed with other covered bridges in the chapter with that name (pp. 217). It's back off the road and is just visible to your left.) Further along on your left, soon after the bridge, is Forest Service (FS) Road 20. This is the beginning of the Siskiyou Loop Drive.

I was introduced to this delightful drive by my uncle one August after a late and snow-filled winter. When we arrived at the summit there were still patches of snow. With just a turn in the road, we had reverted to early spring, and were presented with an array of spring wild flowers. My uncle was a plant enthusiast and knew most plants by both their Latin and common names. He enthusiastically got out of the car to get down on his knees for a closer look at some of the smaller flowers — of course addressing them by name. It remains an endearing memory.

A map will be helpful at this point, for smaller roads lead off into the woods, and it's sometimes hard to tell which branch in the road to follow. Take your time and enjoy the vistas before arriving at Mt. Ashland Ski resort. From there follow the signs back to Ashland.

Other Drives

There are many other longer drives you can take to enjoy a wider look at the area. In another chapter is a description of three **drives to the Pacific Ocean** and the pleasures to see en route and at your destination.

Are you interested in waterfalls? Take State 62 to Crater Lake and continue to Diamond Lake. From there, Highway 138, the highway from Diamond Lake to Roseburg, passes many falls on both sides of the road as it meanders along and crisscrosses the Umpqua River. Some of these falls are at or near the parking lots just off the highway. Others involve hikes of varying lengths. This area is described more fully in the chapter on *Rivers and Waterfall*, (pp. 179). This drive would take a whole day or more to really see its wonders.

Are you fascinated by volcanoes? Again, take State 62 to Crater Lake. You could just stay there and explore the different activities in this National Park. Or you could return to State 140 heading south and drive past Klamath Falls. At the south-end of the lake, look for U.S highway 97 and drive into California. As described in another chapter, *(Caves*, pp. 205), drive to The Lava Beds National Monument. In the process, you get two very different looks at what volcanoes can do and what they leave behind when they become dormant.

Still farther south into California are two other more active volcanoes — Lassen and Shasta. Though neither has erupted much in the last century, they're capable of erupting at any time. Fortunately for humans, they always give warnings that they're thinking about it, so a visit is always safe. There are several places of interest for the visitor at Lassen. There are the fumaroles, boiling springs, boiling lakes, and mud pots, in addition to hiking trails, numerous small cooler lakes, and even small volcanoes and cinder cones with trails to their summits. There's less variety at Shasta, which is popular for serious hiking. (Check with the rangers.)

All of these volcano-oriented meanderings would take more than a day. So you'd have to pick and choose or plan ahead to stay overnight, in order to do it all.

Animals

Those of you who love animals will want to know about several places in Southern Oregon where you can view and/or interact with animals.

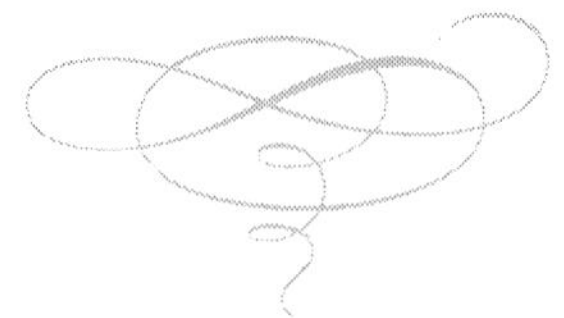

Top of the list of animal places to visit is **Wildlife Images Rehabilitation and Education Center.** Fliers and travel books list its mailing address as in Grants Pass. That may be, but it's really located 12 miles further North/West on the fringes of Merlin.

Directions: The address is 11845 Lower River Road, Grants Pass, OR 97526.

Take the Merlin Road exit (#61) from I-5 and drive about four miles to the community of Merlin. On the far side of town is Robertson Bridge Road. Turn to the left. Drive to Lower River Road (a dead end), and again turn to the left. Wildlife Images is almost immediately on the right.

Wildlife Images Rehabilitation and Educational Center is an institution dedicated to treating injured wild animals — mostly mammals and birds — and returning them to the wilds if their injuries have healed enough for them to care for themselves adequately without human intervention. If this is not the case, the animals become permanent residents and their presence helps instruct the public about their species, joining other animals in the educational aspect of Wildlife Images. One step in the educational process is to have some staff members take these animals to schools — in cages or on leash — to teach the students to respect these beautiful creatures. Students learn the do's and don'ts of interacting with the animals.

Another part of the educational process includes allowing visitors to tour the premises. This doesn't mean allowing people to wander on their own, but instead Wildlife Images offers docent-led guided tours with well-informed volunteer guides. The guides take visitors past many animals in cages or behind fences, instructing about the species and answering visitors' questions.

But the tour doesn't go near recuperating animals. Hopefully these animals will be released soon, and the staff doesn't want the animals to become too comfortable with people. They're safer if they have a healthy fear of humans. In fact, very unfortunately some of the animals become patients because people shot or otherwise wounded them — usually through carelessness but sometimes through cruelty.

Animals in need find their way here in different ways. Many animals are injured by cars, so sometimes a highway patrol officer brings them in (or notifies the staff that there is an animal needing assistance). At other times, private citizens make phone calls to report an injured animal by the road; or residents bring in an injured wild animal they have come across. Sometimes the animals needing care are not injured but orphaned; some are confiscated because they're not legally in the state and are perhaps dangerous; and some are surrendered wild animal "pets" that have grown too big or too hard to manage. A few are former movie animals now living in retirement.

Wildlife Images also keeps on the premises and cares for wild animals that have been cured of their injuries but cannot be returned to the wild — usually because they are either not native to the state (and releasing them would be against the law) or because they have become too humanized. If you're familiar with the Australian Steve Irwin, the Crocodile Hunter, you may remember his wife had adopted a mountain lion that she could not take to Australia when she married and moved there. This animal had become quite humanized and would have had difficulty in living on her own in the wilds and might have been a danger to herself or to human beings. Wildlife Images agreed to take her in, and she lived out her life in this caring facility. Steve and Terry visited Wildlife Images from time to time, forming a sweet relationship with the staff. There's a bench dedicated to him on the front porch of the office.

There's more to discover about this wonderful place. Let me just conclude that we visit every year, always have a different guide, and always learn something different with each guide.

The public may visit daily, by appointment only, basically from 9:30 a.m. through 3 p.m., with tours lasting about an hour and a-half. The paths are paved and accessible to wheelchairs. Children may be included, but parents are asked to keep them in tow, staying with the guide being a must. Questions from all ages are welcome.

Reservations are required in order to control the number of visitors in each group, and there is a fee, $10 as of this printing.

The phone number is 541-476-0222.

Wildlife Safari

Directions: To get there, take I-5 to the Winston exit and follow the signs to Wildlife Safari. There are large animal footprints painted on the road to help guide you.

Note about your car windows: In enclosed areas where there are animals considered dangerous, your windows should always be kept closed. In the more generally fenced area, windows may be open unless there are animals near, in which case close them.

There are several similar Safari zoological parks in other states, such as California, each with wild animals from all over the world, roaming free within a large area surrounded by a high fence. There is an admission fee to drive through the fenced park, and an attendant opens the entrance gate for each car. You may only want to visit the area outside the fence — the visitor center, the area housing small caged animals and reptiles, or the venues where animals are presented in shows, ranging from elephants and jungle cats to birds. That's all pretty standard procedures for this type of park.

The one I'm referring to is a nearly 600-acre park in Winston, near Roseburg. Here, once past the entrance gate, visitors are frequently greeted by a group of ostriches, who might poke their beaks right up to the car's closed windows. Having passed this greeting line, visitors navigate slowly on good gravel roads that meander through wild animals placed for their compatibility and place of origin, with unobtrusive barriers separating those from Africa, Asia, North America, etc. The animals do the natural things such as graze, snooze, or take a leisurely stroll.

Those animals that are deemed dangerous — jungle cats and bears — are kept additionally in smaller fenced and gated areas. A guard opens the gate only when there's a car awaiting entrance, and closes it as soon as the car is within the enclosure. Here visitors are instructed to not stop their cars and to keep their windows closed at all times. I'm sure these are wise precautions, but during the five or six times I've visited, I've rarely seen the cats do anything but sleep, and the bears to take an occasional swim in their pond. I'm also sure obedience to these requirements helps keep the park and these smaller enclosures open and available for human visits. So "no stopping" and "closed windows" it is. And you're allowed to circle through these double fenced areas again.

When you have finished the drive through the larger park area you can drive through this main Safari part again, too, if you please. Or, park your car outside the fenced area in the large parking lot and visit cages and enclosures not behind guarded fences where smaller animal life is displayed — small rodents, snakes, monkeys, and even flamingos. There's a petting zoo with goats, etc., where youngsters and older children and parents may pet and feed these tame animals.

Next to the gift shop is an auditorium where there are daily wild animal shows. Beyond these buildings are bleachers by an arena where there are shows including larger animals like elephants.

This park has concrete paths throughout the pedestrian area and is easily visited by families pushing wheelchairs or strollers. There are a few food dispensaries and a restaurant.

Great Cats World Park

Directions: It's 30 miles southwest of Grants Pass on Redwood Highway (State 199), on the left, 1.2 miles south of Cave Junction.

This wonderful park is on the highway connecting Grants Pass and Crescent City, CA. Look for it just beyond the turn-off to Oregon Caves in Cave Junction, on the left side of the road.

When we visited **Great Cats World Park** there were no large signs announcing the park, so we had to look for it. And neither were there large crowds to get our attention, but the numbers of people in attendance could vary with the day or season. Once we had parked our car, we approached a humble-looking shop and fenced area, and we were delighted with our approximated 1 ½ hour visit.

Like Wildlife Images, visitors do not wander on their own. A group of people is introduced to a guide who is familiar with each of the 15-20 cats — mostly of different species — and will show you each animal's characteristic behaviors. There's usually one cat per enclosure and the guide will typically affectionately call each animal by name, feed it some favorite meat, and then encourage it to stretch tall, roar, or perform some other typical behavior. There are a few bench seats at each stop — some shaded — if periods of standing are difficult for you.

Be ready with questions! The guides love to answer questions.

There's a small area outside the gift shop where you can eat lunch. The visitor can purchase food — as I recall the food was grilled sandwiches or packaged stuff like peanuts or candy from a machine. But the staff apparently has no problem with people who bring their own lunches and enjoy the patio setting to eat.

I've stopped at this park only once, and that was May of 2011, but I liked it so much that I look forward to another visit.

This park would make an interesting stop before or after a visit to the Oregon Caves. They're located quite near each other and provide an interesting contrast.

This venue is closed December and January.

Phone 541-592-2957 if you have questions.

Address: 27919 Redwood Highway, Cave Junction, OR 97523

Hours: March 1 – Oct. 31, daily 11 a.m. – 4:00 p.m. There are extended summer hours, from Memorial Weekend – Labor Day 10:00 a.m. – 6:00 p.m. For off-season hours check the web site at www.greatcatsworldpark.com.

Fees: Adults 13 and up is $14.00, Seniors 65 and up $12.00, Children ages 4-12 $10.00. Ages 3 and under are free.

West Coast Game Park Safari

7 miles south of Bandon on Highway 101

This attraction is south of Coos Bay and west of Coquille. Though quite near the ocean, it is not near enough to see any water.

Directions: It's quite simple. Get to the ocean – to U.S. Highway 101 – any way you choose and aim for Bandon. There are signs advertising this popular park, so once on Hwy 101 just follow their directions.

This is the largest and most interesting petting zoo I've seen. There's a greater variety of animals, and there are interesting up-close sessions with animals you might not otherwise get a chance to stroke. The animals all look healthy and as happy as you could expect with the constant people attention.

To start, I'll just list the animals the flier says live here: African lion, tiger, leopard, snow leopard, cougar, black panther, lynx, bear, monkeys, chimpanzee, binturong, buffalo, elk, deer, llama, camel, zebra, ostrich, fox, sheep, and goats. That's a long list of their more than 450 birds and animals living here in this 21-acre setting. Obviously, not all these animals are people friendly and some remain behind strong fences. In that sense, this is more like a small zoo; but those inhabitants deemed safe, including the usual sheep and goats, are llamas, elk, and deer and others, that wander freely. Trained staff is very much in attendance, circulating among the animals to make sure they're OK with the attention they're getting. As a result, some animals stay out only a short time because the staff sees they've had enough people time and return them to their enclosures. One thing different from other petting zoos I've visited is that some baby animals not usually mixing with humans — such as bears and bobcats — come out for a while in a controlled situation and "suffer themselves to be admired," before retreating.

Our visit was quite pleasant — even fun — as we associated with quite an array of humans of all ages who interacted with the animals. There were a few places you could purchase acceptable food to feed the inhabitants. Oh, and you can take a camel ride — for a fee probably.

Many people were visiting on the day we there, but the parking lot was adequate to handle all the cars. There are several trees, which provided shade for both people and animals alike.

This may be a longer drive than you'd like to make to visit a petting zoo, but if it's not too far for you, give this a try. Everyone I saw was having a wonderful time.

The park is open January through November with varying hours. Phone ahead to check the hours when you're planning a visit. The phone number is 541-347-3106, or check their web site: www.gameparksafari.com.

The North Coast Marine Mammal Rescue Center

Directions: This is in Crescent City and is near the Information Center on H and 6th streets. There's an area along the ocean, between the Information Center and the lighthouse that has a very large, grassy area where people play sports or just play. On the side away from the ocean is this Rescue Center. There is ample parking near the Lighthouse, and the Rescue Center has a smaller parking lot of its own. You could park anywhere around here and walk to several attractions: a viewing spot for the lighthouse that can be visited only at low tide, the Information Center, the Rescue Center, and statuary of historical interest.

The North Coast Marine Mammal Rescue Center is rather small, having about six enclosures. In front of the building, before you enter, is a large sign, which introduces the animals currently being cared for — their breed, size, and the circumstances that brought them here. Also, the center's hours are posted here. Unfortunately, we didn't have the information about the hours before arriving and just missed taking the tour that includes a question-and-answer opportunity. But, fortunately for us, the pens are all outside and easily viewed by those outside the cyclone fence. As we looked at what we could see of the animals, two staff members prepared to feed their charges. One of the ladies came over and talked with us, answering the questions we would have asked on the tour. (By this time, there were about three families gathered around.) We saw how reluctant eaters were gently dealt with and sympathized with them. We also felt good about the others who were doing OK with self-feeding. We found that sea lions and seals have to eat in the water — as they would do in the wild — and the reluctant ones were lovingly nudged with a special board until they dove into the water and ate. The sea lion closest to the cyclone fence was brought to the center by people that were sure his injuries were enough to kill him and thought he wouldn't make it. But the caregivers soon found that there was still life in him and tenderly gave him the attention he so desperately needed — and he is now well on his way to recovery. This is just one of their many success stories.

I wish I could give you their hours and the days open, but none of my sources give that information, not even their web site. However, the gift shop's hours are 11:00 a.m. to 4:00 p.m. I would suggest that visitors come before 3:00 p.m. weekdays. For more complete information, ask at the nearby Information Center.

Dogs for the Deaf in Central Point

10175 Wheeler Road

This attraction is at the foot of Table Rock Mountain.

Directions: Take exit #33 from I-5. Turn right at the stop light and left onto Table Rock Road. Pass Tou Velle Park and pass the Rogue River Ranch and look for milepost #10. Turn left on Wheeler Road. (You'll see the sign for Dogs for the Deaf at the corner of Wheeler and Table Rock Road.) Continue on Wheeler Road about ¼ mile and turn left into the parking lot.

Dogs trained at this center are not chosen because of their breed but because of the characteristics they manifest, such as gentleness, patience, and alertness. The dogs are "rescue dogs" and come from shelters where they might otherwise be put down. Once chosen, these rescue dogs are taught by professional trainers the skills needed to help people with various disabilities, especially those with hearing problems. Tours are available by appointment that show the skills the dogs have learned. It's about an hour tour, and experience has shown that small children get bored soon, so children under 5 are generally not allowed.

One of the first things on the agenda of a visit is to view a video showing just what the staff does here. You see some segments dealing with training, and others showing the dogs in their adopted homes — both interesting and heartwarming. Then during our visit, at some point there came a knock at the door, and a staff member brought in a young trainee. This dog demonstrated some of the skills he was learning. Since he's still learning, he made a few mistakes. Actually, it was pretty cute.

After this part of the program, the group was led to a place to view the kennels on the lower floor and then upstairs where further training took place in rooms the staff had arranged to look like someone's home.

In all it was a pleasant visit.

Dogs for the Deaf request that you **please phone ahead for reservations.** This is to make sure that there are not too many people in each session. There's no fee, but donations are gratefully accepted.

The hours are May 1 – Sept. 30, Monday – Friday, 10:00 a.m., 11:00 a.m., 1:00 p.m., and 2:00 p.m.

Oct. 1 – April 30 there are tours at 10:00 a.m. and 2:00 p.m.

The phone number is 541-826-9220.

US Fish and Wildlife Forensic Laboratory

A reminder: This business — sharing the parking area for the Ashland Scienceworks Museum — is not open to the public. It's a working place, and visitors would definitely be in the way. Since there were no definitive signs outside, when we knocked on the door to make inquiries, the staff member was polite but firm — no visitors.

Sports

We'll be driving around the area to enjoy more of what Mother Nature has to offer, but first let's take a break for some physical activity.

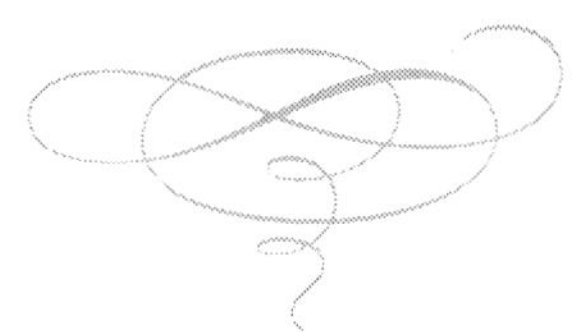

Medford and Ashland have opportunities for many participant sports activities. Most of them are in Medford.

Swimming

There are swimming pools in both cities. Medford has Hawthorne Park and Jackson Park, as well as the YMCA. Ashland provides pools at Meyer Daniel Pool, 1705 Homes, and Well Springs, 2253 Hwy 99. Their YMCA is also open to the public and offers swimming as well as other sports activities. (If you have a hometown membership, be sure to bring your Y membership card. Non-members pay a fee for each day use.) In addition, there is recreational swimming — really, more like play — at most motels. Some of the numerous lakes and streams are deep enough for swimming and not just wading.

Rowing

If you're interested in rowing and related activities, it's here. Check with the information listed in this book under Emigrant Lake or in the chapter *Water Activities in Southern Oregon*, (pp. 143.)

Tennis

There are tennis courts at Medford's Bear Creek Park, Holmes Park, and Union Park as well as many public schools in both Ashland and Medford.

Golf

I'm not a golfer, so I can't tell you which of the following golf courses is the best, or if any of them are closed to all but members, but I list them for your convenience should you be interested. Oak Knoll is the only one in Ashland.

- Bear Creek Golf Course – Medford – 541-773-1822
- Eagle Point Golf Course – Medford – 541-826-8225
- Laurel Hill Golf Course –Medford – 541-855-7965
- Oak Knoll Golf Course – Ashland – 541-482-4311
- Quail Point Golf Course – Medford – 541-857-7000
- Rogue Valley Country Club – Medford – 541-772-4050
- Stewart Meadows Golf – Medford – 541-770-6554
- Stone Ridge Golf Course – Medford – 541-830-4653

Hiking

Many local, county, state, and national parks or monuments have hiking trails. Check in the chapter on *Parks in Southern Oregon*, (pp. 149) for those that specify this activity. Since hiking is such a popular sport, trails are everywhere. If you walk the roads in the undeveloped portion of Lithia Park, you find yourself hiking in lovely, natural space. The trail in Medford called Bear Creek Greenway has a paved surface and is a few miles long. Used by both bikers and hikers, its parallel and adjacent to I-5 and is accessed at Barnett road in the south or Table Rock Road in the north. There are hiking opportunities at Mount Ashland and in the hills across the valley. Hiking is so prevalent that if you go where the scenery looks pleasing to you, you'll probably find hiking trails. Some specific hiking trails are at the locations listed below.

Table Rock Mountain

Directions: Leave I-5 at exit #30. Take Hwy 99 north of Medford to Table Rock Road and turn to the right. The road goes over the overpass crossing I-5. Drive toward the monoliths until you come to the base of these formations, about 10 miles from I-5 at Wheeler Road. Here there is a large sign advertising Dogs for the Deaf. Turn to the left and drive about .5 miles to a right bend in the road at the "Dogs" barn. After the bend, drive another .5 mile to a group of rural mailboxes on the right and a parking lot for the trail on the left. (There are signs directing you to this parking, but they're easily missed.)

When you reach the parking lot provided for hikers, there is a roofed-over sign announcing Lower Table Rock Preserve, with a list of precautions, including loose rocks, deep crevices, poison oak, and rattlesnakes. As of our last visit, there are no restrooms or drinking fountains. The start of the trail is a gravel road, and you're asked to stay on the trail, rather than cross-country exploring on these privately owned lands.

There are actually two mesas quite near each other, and one is clearly viewed from I-5 heading north. These monuments are named Upper Table Rock and Lower Table Rock, the latter being the one you see from I-5. Upper Table Rock has more sloping sides than its partner and the top isn't so flat, but its size is almost twice that of Lower Table Rock. Upper Table Rock is nearly horseshoe shaped and has a hiking trail to the summit. (We were advised that if we chose to hike to the top we should take a large stick, because rattlesnakes love the top on a nice, warm summer day.) Few trees grow on or near either mesa, and the hike will probably be quite hot. A water canteen of some sort would undoubtedly be welcome equipment.

Smaller Lower Table Rock, with two giant monoliths comprising its façade, is the prettier of the two, in my eyes. Interestingly, it has a landing strip on its top, which is even marked on some maps. We were told that since the length is shorter than the distance usually needed for takeoff, the last part of takeoff involves a rather exciting drop before the plane soars into flight.

If you're an avid hiker always looking for a new view, these two trails would be interesting possibilities. Also, if you're a rock hound or a geologist intrigued with the mesas, you could conceivably find these irresistible. An added bonus on these hikes and the drive to the parking lot is a wonderful view of Mt. McLoughlin.

Boundary Springs

This hike is a part of the Crater Lake experience, so follow State 62 toward Crater Lake. When you get to the turnoff for the Lake, stay on State 62 and drive another few miles to the large parking lot on the right which is provided for those wanting a long-distance view of the crater or seeking to read the plaques giving information about the formation of the crater. This is also the head of the trail going down to the Boundary Springs, the beginnings of the Rogue River.

When hiking this trail, described as medium difficulty, be advised that mosquitoes love this area. Our first attempt to find the springs was aborted when I found myself being eaten alive by the mosquitoes, blood running down one leg. The next year we arrived with long pants, long-sleeved shirts, real shoes instead of sandals, and insect spray. So prepared, we had no difficulty.

Near the beginning, the walk took us past a large number of pines flopped on their sides much like pick-up sticks (apparently the result of a long-ago wind storm). We soon got down to a small stream crossed by two perhaps eight feet long logs cut in half. This gentle stream was the mighty Rogue in its infancy. A little further along, the trail came to a dirt road, a part of Hamaker

Campground. After crossing the road, the path wound through ferns and trees before reaching a spot of gushing water, and the trail ended. There was no identifying sign, but it was clear we had reached the Boundary Spring.

A faster route is to find the signs to Hamaker Campground along State 62, turn in, and start hiking from their parking lot, skipping the mosquitoes.

In all, I'm glad I took both routes to get to the springs, thoroughly enjoying both trips. Along the way there were many picture opportunities. Though the longer route is somewhere around three miles round trip, neither walk is arduous, and children may enjoy it.

Grizzly Peak

This peak is nearly 6,000 feet above and across the valley from Ashland.

Directions: To get there, take State 66 out of town, cross I-5, and proceed beyond the motels. After the road has curved, there is a road called Dead Indian Memorial Road. (The word "dead" is sometimes omitted.) Turn left and drive about 6.5 miles to Shale City Road — marked "38-2E-27." Drive another couple of miles, gaining altitude. You'll soon see signs directing you to the Grizzly Peak Trail.

This is a wide and well-cared-for trail of about 3.5 miles round trip. You zigzag through a forest of firs and pines, which provide cool shade.

Once at the top you have grand views of the valley and Ashland. This trail, uphill the first half, is not a difficult hike. Children would possibly enjoy it.

Gin Lin Mining Trail

Directions: Drive to Jacksonville and go right through town on the main street until the road curves and becomes State 238. Stay on State 238. At the small town of Ruch, turn to the right on Upper Applegate Road. After passing McKee Covered Bridge, which is on the left, look on the right for Palmer Creek Road and the sign identifying Gin Lin Mining Trail.

This trail takes you back to gold-mining days. Named for a Chinese immigrant gold-miner of the late 1800's, the ¾ mile round trip trail is mostly level. There are trail pamphlets — free if you return yours to the box after your walk — describing the mining processes used here, such as hydraulic mining, the practice of using hoses with nozzles to wash away a hillside to expose the gold nuggets and flakes. The hike is short, easy, educational, and mostly in the shade. Children could easily hike it. But this dirt path is just uneven enough to make it difficult for a wheelchair to navigate.

Mt. McLoughlin

The before-mentioned hikes are short and fairly easy. This hike is not short and easy. The hike up this beautiful peak is described as rough and steep. The 10-mile round trip is challenging both uphill and down, and would take the better part of a day, even for the experienced hiker. You ascend some 4,000 feet. It is recommended to bring "plenty of water, snacks, and sunscreen" plus sunglasses and a walking stick.

If you're wondering if I've ever hiked this trail, the answer is no. I've hiked several trails including Grizzly Peak and Gin Lin, but not this one. The above quote is from one who has hiked there.

Directions: My maps are not clear about how to get there, so checking with a ranger station will give you more help. However, I understand that to get to the trail you should start with State Hwy 62, and turn off at State 140. Shortly after Fish Lake, look for road 3650, which should take you to the trailhead. From there you have to walk — no cars, bikes, or horses are allowed.

Serious hiking is available many places in Southern Oregon, but since most of them would take more time than this book covers, I mention only Mt. McLoughlin as a longer and more difficult hike. The most serious hiking I know of within easy distance of Ashland is at **Mt. Shasta** in Northern California. This is *very* serious hiking, sometimes including climbing using special equipment. Consult a ranger about the advisability of hiking this peak with its weather on any given day, even mid-summer. Weather can change dramatically and quickly. I doubt you would be interested in attending a play after such a hike.

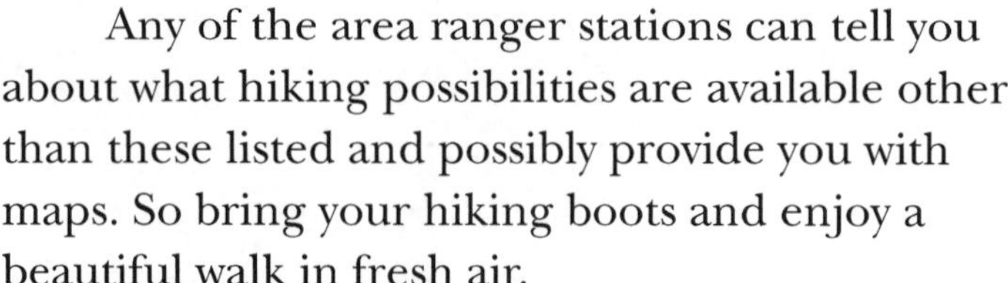

Any of the area ranger stations can tell you about what hiking possibilities are available other than these listed and possibly provide you with maps. So bring your hiking boots and enjoy a beautiful walk in fresh air.

Ice Skating

Darex Family Ice Rink is open only in the winter. If you're here in the summer their phone is not connected. But should you be here November through February, the rink is located at the corner of Winburn Way and Nutley in Ashland near Lithia Park.

Spectator Sports

Horse Racing

Directions: Take I-5 to Grants Pass, State 199 exit #55. Drive through town, and when you see the YMCA on your right, you've arrived. The Downs is adjacent and behind.

Grants Pass Downs is the location for horse racing. It's located at the County Fair Grounds on State 199, races occurring late spring through July 7th, Friday, Saturday, and Sunday. When nearing the location, look for the YMCA building closer to the highway. The fair grounds are set back from the road.

Near the end of June, there is a quarter-horse show in the same location.

Medford As Baseball Team

Location was on State 99.

There was an AAA Oakland Athletics team in Medford. At that time if you were a baseball nut and were here between June and August, you could check with the box office for the schedule and fit in a game. Many of the players were up-and-coming athletes just out of college. It's here that Jose Canseco made his debut, and you could possibly see a future star getting his first taste of professional ball. Occasionally, a more seasoned player has come here to work out some problem, or to get back in shape after an injury.

Unfortunately, the "franchise" was moved to another location. So you can't see the A's here anymore, but there is an effort underway to bring in another similar team. Check on-line under Medford Baseball for information. If there is a team, its location may be here at the old AAA Oakland Athletics' field, which is a county park. Good luck!

Incidentally, we attended a night game here a few years back, and it had a rather small town atmosphere, with many of the fans being nearly as interested in each other as they were in the game. Also, the announcer was telling a whole lot more about the raffle of the inning than he was about the game. The atmosphere made me think a bit of my hometown's industrial league baseball games. However, the players showed their skill, and it was a pretty good

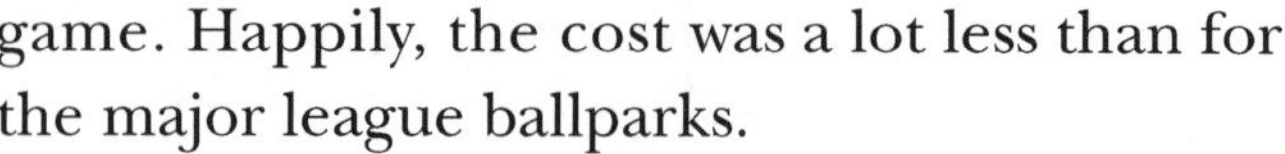

game. Happily, the cost was a lot less than for the major league ballparks.

Soccer

Check with www.ashlandsoccer.com for a schedule and location of games, for they vary.

Miscellany

There are also new sports complexes in the Medford area that offer racquetball, bowling, and roller-skating. You can find tracks for off-road vehicles, sports cars, go-carts, and motorcycles at the **Jackson County Sports Park**. To get there take State 62 to State 140 to Kershaw Road. It's 13 miles NE of Medford near White City.

In summary, I know there must be other sports activities, and if there's a special one you like, they undoubtedly have it. For further information, check the Information Centers, the local phonebooks, or (if you have access to a computer) on-line.

Water Activities in Southern Oregon

There's lots of water in Southern Oregon — lakes and reservoirs, rivers and creeks, and water falls. There's also a long stretch of beaches at the ocean, which is covered in the chapter called *A Day at the Beaches*, (pp. 223).

It would be silly to have all that water and not take advantage of it, so there are several recreational water activities available: You can swim nearly everywhere there's water; river rafting is abundantly advertised; fishing is plentiful; and water skiing is possible on some larger lakes or reservoirs. If you're into rowing, there is a website giving information. In short, if there's a water activity that interests you, you can probably find it. Here are some details.

There are countless opportunities to **swim**. For a quick dip when you have virtually no time, there is, of course, your motel. If you want to swim laps there is the local YMCA where visitors are welcome. (If you're a member of your hometown Y, bring your membership card and ID with you. You can have 10 free visits a year. **Non-members are also welcome — for a $10 fee for each visit** as of this writing). When my uncle swam for therapeutic reasons, Southern Oregon University allowed him to use one of their lap pools.

Swimming for any reason — exercise, therapy, recreation, or simply to cool down — is possible many places; but in general, when you're not in a city and come across some inviting water, if there's no sign prohibiting swimming, you're welcome to do so. There are many lakes and streams where swimming is encouraged, and in the following three chapters I list some of them: *Lakes; Rivers and Waterfalls; and Parks.*

But what other water activities are there?

Ride a River. River rafting is available on a couple of different levels, from white-water rafting to the more leisurely rides that introduce you to back-woods areas not easily reached in cars. White-water rafting inevitably will bounce you around a bit and get you wet. Even these rides differ in the level of exertion and length of trip, from half a day to several days (combined with camping). During some parts of the year a few of these trips include fishing. One basic consideration is whether getting wet and getting bounced around bothers you. Another factor is time. Would a longer trip ruin your schedule? If either answer is "yes," then you might want to try a shorter, more sedate trip.

We elected to test the shorter calm water trips because of the time issue.

Directions: To get to the start of your ride, follow the directions given you by the company you've chosen for your ride. I know there is a large operation across the Rogue River from Riverside Park in Grants Pass, but I'm sure there are others. Probably all companies will give you maps or pamphlets that show you how to get there.

The boat for our ride was powered by a water jet, and we rarely felt a drop or a splash. Unless it's a cool day you won't want or need a sweater to keep warm. On a hot day you may want some sun protection — a hat or some sun block, for instance.

At the time we took the ride there were two daily trips: 10:00 a.m. and 1:30 p.m., each a scant two hours in length — but check with jet-boat companies for their current schedules. The ride covered 34 miles round trip, jet boating to about a mile from the city of Gold Hill. Our pilot, who was also our guide, made frequent stops for a photo op or to point out places of interest. We learned about the history of that stretch of river and many nature facts. Our tour left promptly at 10:00 a.m. and included seniors to small children. Traveling about 25-30 miles an hour, this was not a fast trip, but was relaxing and pleasant.

There are a few advantages to these calmer rides. As noted, they take less time. And obviously, if you don't want to get tossed around or get wet, this would be the type of ride to take. Also, these rides are partly educational in nature. As a bonus, some of the driver/guides may provide you with a few chuckles or even laughs along the way; our driver was somewhat of a comedian!

A different type of ride is later in the day, at 5:00 p.m., when a **dinner ride** departs. This is a four-hour round-trip excursion, possibly leaving from the same dock. Dinner is not served on the boat, but they deliver you to a restaurant riverside for a pleasant repast before returning you to the dock.

All these rides are popular, and seating is limited to boat capacity — about 15 people in our case. Whichever type ride or company you choose, **be sure to phone for reservations a day or two ahead of time**. (At least one rafting company picks you up in Ashland, while other companies expect to greet you at the dock.) So decide how much time you have, choose your level of intensity, make your reservations, and have a good time.

If you have your own boat and want to put it in the water, Evans Perry Park under the bridge at Rogue River City — the one crossing the river under I-5 — includes a boat ramp and some picnic tables, many of which are in the shade of large trees. The park has smaller trees and little plots of gardens planted by various local service organizations. Since this area has been hit by devastating winter floods a few times, these gardens could well be replacement plantings. At any rate, it was a pleasant place to picnic. Other activities here include swimming and fishing. Restrooms are provided.

A historical note: Evans Perry Park also called Coyote Evans Wayside is at the location of a now-defunct ferry service dating back to 1851. And incidentally, Evans Perry Park is one of the many places where we found memorial monuments or plaques to veterans of wars dating back to WWI. Southern Oregonians are very patriotic.

Some water recreational activities demand more of the individual than these low-level boat rides, such as **waterskiing, fishing**, and r**owing. Scuba diving** is also a possibility at the ocean.

Waterskiing is allowed in most lakes big enough to accommodate the long runs desirable in this sport. Howard Prairie Lake, Diamond Lake, and Applegate Reservoir are three that come to mind.

Fishing is popular on many of the streams and at parks. Information for the best spots for both of these activities is available at the ranger station in Ashland on State 66 just before it crosses I-5. It's on the right side of the road just before the Arco station. Look for their small brown sign. There are also Information Centers in several cities that have knowledgeable staffs and provide maps, much as the rangers do. I include some information about where to fish in the chapter titled *Parks*, (pp. 149).

If you're into **rowing**, it's available. For information about what's specifically available, contact the Ashland Rowing Club. To quote them, "The Ashland Rowing Club is a non-profit organization open to anyone 12 and older, offering recreational and competitive outdoor and indoor rowing." They row year round on Emigrant Lake, just outside Ashland. For additional information about the Rowing Club, here's their website: www.ashlandrowingclub.org/.

If I've left out your favorite water activity, ask at an Information Center. It may be available.

Parks in Southern Oregon

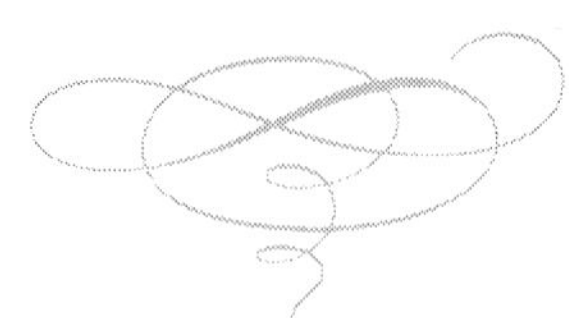

Jackson County Parks

There are many lovely and diverse parks in and near Jackson County, run by the county or the state. Several have something unique — such as a covered bridge (McKee Bridge at the Applegate Bridge Wayside and discussed in the chapter *Covered Bridges,* pp. 217) or a festival (Britt in Jacksonville). Many of them are at a lake or river location, others are in forests, and most provide picnic tables and some sort of restroom facilities. I've visited many of them and will share my observations where I have something additional to contribute. We found most of them to be great places for some downtime, especially if you're traveling with children.

In all, Jackson County has 16 county parks, some of them only minimally developed and lacking some facilities helpful to the visitor. First, here is a list of the parks with their locations.

A. Agate Lake – Off Hwy 140 on Antelope Rd., 14 miles NE of Medford
B. Applegate Bridge Wayside (McKee Covered Bridge) – on Hwy 238, 24 miles SW of Medford.
C. Britt Gardens – in Jacksonville, near California St. and First St.
D. Cantrall-Buckley Park – Off Hwy 238 on Hamilton Road, 8 miles SW of Jacksonville
E. Coyote Evans and Fleming – Off I-5 on Rogue River in the city of Rogue River, 21 miles W of Medford

F. Dodge Bridge – On Rogue River near Highways 234 and 62, 16 miles NW of Medford
G. Emigrant Lake – Off Hwy 66, five miles SE of Ashland
H. Hoover Ponds – South of Hwy 140 between Lake View Dr. and Kershaw Rd., 11 Miles NE of Medford.
I. Howard Prairie Lake – Off Hwy 66 on Howard Prairie Rd., 25 miles NE of Ashland
J. Jackson County Sports Park – Off Hwy 140 on Kershaw Rd., 13 Miles NE of Medford
K. Miles Field – On Hwy 99 near Phoenix
L. Palmerton Park – On Evans Creek and W. Evans Creek Rd.,1/2 mile NW of city of Rogue River
M. Rogue Elk Park – On Hwy 62 and Rogue River, 27 miles North of Medford
N. Savage Rapids Park – On Hwy 99 and Savage Creek, 3 miles W of city of Rogue River
O. Shady Cove Park – On Hwy 62 and Rogue River, 21 miles N of Medford
P. Willow Lake – Off Butte Falls-Fish Lake Rd, 7 ½ miles SW of Butte Falls

Agate Lake is first alphabetically, not in importance. The brochure says that Agate Lake offers a picnic area, vault toilets, and a boat ramp. You can use boats powered by wind (as in sailboats), oars (as in canoes and row boats), and electricity, but not motorboats. You can also fish and swim here. Non-water sports include archery, radio-controlled airplanes, and baseball.

We visited there in the hottest time of summer, and all we saw was barren land surrounding a waterhole. We saw none of the sports activities listed, but they may be found at other seasons. It was perhaps the most uninviting space we've visited in Southern Oregon, with no shade and no drinking water in sight, though a pit toilet was available. The only tree was dead, a somewhat interesting skeleton. There was one family fishing from the bank. I called the County Parks Office to inquire about the park and was told that it's well-used, popular for fishing and slow boating. We must have visited at the wrong time.

Applegate Bridge Wayside is better known to us as **McKee Covered Bridge Wayside.** This park is for day use only and it offers picnic tables, vault toilets, swimming, fishing, and horseshoe pits.

This is a favorite spot that we've visited many times. To get there, drive through Jacksonville — itself a historic park-like spot, discussed in another chapter (pp. 73). Keep driving on Main Street until it goes beyond Jacksonville and becomes Highway 238. When you get to the small town of Ruch, take the right "Y" in the road, staying on Hwy 238. You will pass the Star Ranger Station almost immediately. There is a sign to Cantrall-Buckley Park, which we'll mention later. Keep on Hwy 238 looking for a small sign announcing **McKee Bridge** and an arrow pointing to the left. Having turned left, you'll see the bridge.

This bridge is restricted to pedestrians now, and is kept in good condition. A bronze plaque tells its history. One year when we were visiting, there was a woman sitting by the bridge soliciting money to repair Oregon's covered bridges. We found she was a member of the McKee family and was happy to talk about their history. Wonderful serendipity! And, yes, we happily made a donation.

The Wayside itself has been left in a rather natural state, with no lawn. It has individual picnic tables plus a gazebo providing cover for more tables and a large-group barbeque pit. On the level with the tables is a "sluice," a small flowing sort of canal, a leftover of gold mining times. To get to the river, you descend stone steps near the sluice. Having descended you find the Applegate River is of varying depths. On one side it's shallow enough for toddlers to wade. On the other bank it's deep enough for diving off the ledge on the cliff above.

This is a popular area. We always see families with young children playing in the water.

There are vault toilets and some spigots that provide drinking water. At the entrance to the park is a small general-purpose store where you could buy some simple supplies.

See chapter on *Covered Bridges* for more details (pp. 217).

Britt Gardens is in the city of Jacksonville and is discussed there (pp. 77). It's a wonderful outside venue for musical presentations under the stars.

Cantrall-Buckley Park is not far from McKee Covered Bridge Park. This park is located on the Applegate River off Hwy 238 on Hamilton Road, eight miles southwest of Jacksonville. It offers picnicking, camping, a group reservation area, restrooms, showers, swimming, fishing, an interpretive display, and hiking trails.

This is an inviting park with a grassy area around stately trees. It's right on the river, and not far from the highway.

Coyote Evans and Fleming Park is located on the Rogue River off I-5 in the city of Rogue River, 21 miles west of Medford. It's for day use only. It has a picnic area, a boat ramp, swimming, and fishing.

This park is right under the large bridge that crosses I-5 at the exit to the city. While very small, the park is green and cool most of the summer. During the winter it's been hit by flooding many times. The young plants tell me they've been replaced recently.

Local service clubs show the area's patriotic feelings by providing some plaques honoring war veterans.

Other than picnic tables, restrooms and the dock, there are few manmade amenities here; it's just a restful spot in a beautiful setting. Street-side there's an information building.

Dodge Bridge Park is located on the Rogue River on Highway 234 (which goes through Sam's Valley) near Hwy 62 and is 16 miles northwest of

Medford. It's for day use only. There's a picnic area, vault toilets, a boat ramp, and you can fish, swim, and raft.

Rogue Elk Park, located on the Rogue River on Hwy 62, 27 miles north of Medford is much the same type of park, additionally offering camping sites and restroom/showers. There are also hiking trails.

Emigrant Lake is located off Hwy 66, five miles southeast of Ashland. It's viewable from I-5 as you approach the city.

Emigrant Lake is a sort of horseshoe-shaped reservoir, about 15 minutes from downtown Ashland, under the gentle watch of Mt. Ashland in low hills south and east of town. A few trees dot the hills around the lake, but basically it's a pretty sunny place. If you burn easily, take note.

This recreational area offers all water-related activities, such as swimming, fishing, boating (including both sail and motor), rowing, water-skiing, and windsurfing. There's even a waterslide — 280-foot, twin flumed. There are areas for picnicking and camping for both small and large groups. Amenities include dressing rooms and showers. There are volleyball courts, horseshoe pits, and a baseball diamond. Concessions include a laundry, the waterslide and pool, jet-ski rental, and fast-food refreshments. If you prefer to pick up a lunch before entering the park, there's a small grocery store/deli outside the entrance. Emigrant Lake's public restrooms look pretty decent.

A band shell and platform have been built at lake's edge for concerts. The location is a natural amphitheater with a grassy slope where the audience sits. On summer evenings, entertainers (many well-known) perform for your joy. July 4 celebrations here include spectacular fireworks.

One hot morning we put our inflatable rubber boat in the water and, staying close to the shore, weren't bothered by faster boats. There are boat ramps, but the non-sandy beaches have gentle slopes, and we could launch just about any place we could park. Being there in the morning, perhaps we missed crowds of people that prefer afternoon recreation; but in years with sufficient rainfall, the lake is large enough to accommodate just about all comers.

This park charges an entrance fee for day use.

If you want to get out of the city for lake activities, you can't beat this for convenience. This is not an Alpine lake, but it's very wet!

Howard Prairie Lake is an Alpine Lake, located off Highway 66 on Hyatt-Howard Prairie Road, 25 miles northeast of Ashland. It offers picnicking, camping, a group reservation area with sheltered area for cooking and sleeping, restrooms, showers, boat ramps, marina, a store, restaurant, gas station, fishing, swimming, sailing, water skiing, and hiking. One hiking trail links with the Pacific Crest Trail.

As you approach the lake you see a large barn off to the left and a view of Mt. McLoughlin. This barn is in an equestrian area, which includes corrals, horse trails, and a cross-country jumping course.

Howard Prairie Lake is in a park-like setting and is included in the chapter describing a drive you can take to pass by several beautiful lakes (pp. 105). Howard Prairie is also mentioned in many reference books and pamphlets on Southern Oregon, and rightly so: it's not hard to get to, it has a refreshingly pleasant temperature on hot days, and it's beautiful. We visit often, not to swim, boat or hike, but just to relax and admire.

Jackson County Sports Park is located off Highway 140 and also Kershaw Road, not far from Agate Lake. It's 13 miles northeast of Medford, and is for day use only.

This sports park is just what the name suggests, having 10 Little League/softball fields, racetracks, a shooting range, and fishing ponds. The full list sounds like a rather complete catalog of sports venues: there are motorized vehicle activities, a drag strip, an off-road vehicle track, a mini-bike area, a kart track, and a motorcycle track. They also have firearm ranges: big and small bore, a police and hunter safety range, and a covered sight-in range.

If you're interested in participation sports it sounds as if you'll find it here. For the most current schedule information, call the park's office at 541-776-7001.

Palmerton Park, located on Evans Creek Road, ½ mile northwest of the City of Rogue River, includes an arboretum in addition to picnicking, fishing, and swimming. If you're interested in plant culture you may want to visit.

Rogue Elk Park, located on Hwy 62 near Lost Creek Lake, 27 miles north of Medford, has the usual assortment of activities: picnicking, camping, fishing, swimming, a boat ramp, rafting, and hiking trails. They also provide restrooms and showers.

Shady Cove Park is located nearby on Hwy 62, six miles closer to Medford, following the Rogue River. This is for day use only and provides a picnic area, a boat ramp, and toilets. You can fish, raft, and swim here.

Willow Lake is located 7 ½ miles southeast of Butte Falls on Butte Falls-Fish Lake Road. This park offers picnicking, camping, boat ramps, a marina and store, and a gas station. You can swim, fish, boat, sail, water-ski, and hike.

This is another in the Mountain Lakes Drive (pp. 105). Like Howard Prairie Lake it has an Alpine-like beauty, with evergreen trees in abundance, right down to water's edge.

On the near horizon is a close-up view of Mt. McLoughlin. Undoubtedly, some of the hiking trails lead up this lovely extinct volcano. But remember that hikes on this mountain are described as vigorous and better for the experienced hiker than a family with small children.

Forests

Near Ashland and northwest of Medford is the Rogue River National Forest. While not a park itself, there are several parks within it, such as McKee Covered Bridge, Fish Lake, and all the area around Crater Lake. There are four Ranger Districts, each of which has parks. Some of these parks are for camping, with designated tent sites and the amenities of some sort of toilet, picnic tables, and drinking water. The ranger stations will provide current maps showing where these parks are and how to get there. The closest ranger station is in Ashland, 645 Washington St., near I-5.

There's pleasure in just getting off into the forest and finding a quiet spot to relax. You'll find a variety of trees and shrubs, wildlife, and the sounds of nature — particularly the birds and bubbling water. Elements of this setting will likely refresh you, and taking a short walk will undoubtedly invigorate you.

National and State Parks

Crater Lake National Park is perhaps the most well-known of these parks and is the only National Park in Oregon. It's a caldera of Mt. Mazama, a volcano that blew its top in a cataclysmic explosion before recorded time, and since then has filled with crystal-clear water. This water has its source largely from melting snow and is cold. There are few water activities here, though you may take a guided boat ride around the lake and learn a bit of the geological and natural history. On our tour the guide stopped at one of the small waterfalls at the edge and collected a refreshing drink.

This 1 ¾ hour tour starts at Cleetwood Cove Dock, almost exactly across the lake from the Visitor Center, where the entrance road joins the rim drive. The trail down to the lake at Cleetwood Cove is steep; remember that what goes down eventually comes back up and feels steeper on the ascent! This trail is not recommended for those with respiratory or ambulatory problems. But if you can manage it and have the time, the boat tour is interesting.

If you elect instead to take the 33-mile rim drive, you'll have wonderful and changing views of the lake, some at parking pullouts and some involving short hikes. You'll have frequent opportunities to view the islands in the lake, Wizard Island and Phantom Ship. The hiking trails are usually neither long nor steep. But know your limitations.

Surrounding the lake are mountain peaks, some of which are named.

Allow as much time as pleases you to enjoy this spectacular park. We found that we wanted to spend nearly the whole day here, which meant that to do other things in the area we needed to make another trip from Ashland. Since it's a pretty drive, the only drawback was the gasoline expenditure. Another choice might be to plan a few days here and stay in local lodging.

Mount Lassen National Park

Read details of this park in the Chapter on *Northern California*, (pp. 251).

Mount Shasta National Forest

This snowcapped mountain with an elevation of 14,162 feet is clearly visible from I-5 as you drive south soon after you leave Ashland. Its height also makes it visible from a distance of over 100 miles, seen driving north on a clear day.

That snow lasting through the summer is actually a few glaciers. There's more information about Mt. Shasta also in the chapter on *Northern California*, (pp. 251).

Tou Velle State Park

Another lovely park is **Tou Velle State Park** on the Rogue River on Table Rock Road near the Table Rock mesas. This road divides the park into two sections, one with a ramp for use as a boat launching area, plus parking for boats, boat trailers, and cars. There's nice landscaping, some picnic tables, and restrooms.

The major part of the park is on the other side of the road. Here, after a left turn into the park, you pass an entrance booth where you pay for day use. Once inside the park, you find a more spacious area with manicured lawns, weeping willows, and stately shade trees, picnicking for small and large groups, abundant parking, larger restrooms, and enough space for volleyball and other organized games. In this area the park's road winds gently through grassy plots dotted with large trees. The Rogue River is very shallow here, water barely reaching the hips of adults wading in the middle of the stream. An asphalt walking path follows the water, making easy passage for a wheelchair, and there are occasional benches to stop and enjoy the scenery. You may see a youngster using a rope tied to a tree at river's edge swing out over the water, let go, and splash everything in range. All in all, it's a pleasant environment in a lovely setting. We've visited a few times. For further information see the chapter on *Drives,* (pp. 103).

Oregon Caves National Monument

For information see the chapter named *Caves,* (pp. 205).

Joseph P. Stewart Recreation and State Park

This park is adjacent to Hwy 62 as you drive to Crater Lake. It's a part of the Lost Creek Lake offerings. You can picnic in one area and camp in another. Most water activities are allowed, including swimming, boating, and fishing.

There are also bicycling trails. Restrooms are available.

Tule Lake

For information about Klamath Basin National Wildlife Refuge, including the one at Tule Lake, see the chapter named *Northern California,* (pp. 251).

Lava Beds National Monument

For information about the Lava Beds, see the chapter named *Caves,* (pp. 205).

Lakes

One of the things that make Southern Oregon and Northern California so beautiful is the abundance of water — lakes (natural and manmade), rivers, and waterfalls.

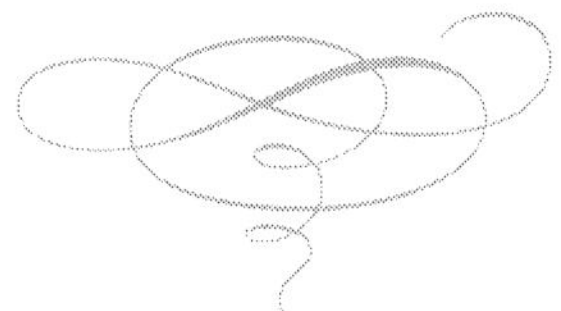

One could take a different drive every day for a few weeks and each day visit a new selection of these lovely sights. But let's start with lakes. Along the way you'll see some streams, but we'll focus on the lakes here and on main rivers and falls later.

Mountain Lakes Drive

There are several beautiful lakes near Ashland, and a lovely drive I've called "Mountain Lakes Drive" will pass by most of them. I've described this favorite route as the second of three drives in the chapter titled *Drives,* (pp. 105). The lakes included are Emigrant, Howard Prairie, Hyatt, Lake of the Woods, Fish Lake, Four Mile Lake, and Willow.

Depending on your reason for taking this drive, you could cover all these lakes in one day or visit them one or two at a time. If you're simply interested in seeing the scenery — including a picnic — you could enjoy them all on a leisurely day. If you wish to add swimming, boating, or fishing, probably one lake is all you'll want. If the latter is your plan, perhaps you'll want to take parts of this trip several different times and enjoy many of these lakes.

All the lakes on this drive provide picnic tables and restrooms plus boat ramps, and you can swim and fish in all of them. Most have small stores where you can buy a snack or a cool drink. These stores also rent fishing equipment and make arrangements for small boat rentals. You could plan a lunch at one of the picnic areas, or come for lunch or dinner in one of the restaurants at a few of the lakes.

The following remarks are true of all the lakes except for Emigrant Lake and Fish Lake. For the others typically the water is crystal clear, and the woods surrounding the lakes come down to water's edge, increasing the lovely views. Also, the cooler air is especially welcome on a hot Ashland or Medford day.

Emigrant Lake

Emigrant is the closest to Ashland, (it's only a few minutes from downtown Ashland) and for that reason it sees the most visitors. It provides a large variety of water activities, and it's certainly very wet, if that's basically all you want. It's neither the prettiest nor the coolest lake. For pretty and cool you'll need to get higher in elevation and under the shade of conifers that the other lakes provide.

To continue on this exploration of lakes, return to State 66, go back to Dead Indian Memorial Road, and turn right. Look for the "Mountain Lakes" sign.

Howard Prairie Lake

The first lake after Emigrant is **Howard Prairie Lake,** which is 17 miles from Ashland. As you approach the lake you get your first view of snow-topped **Mt. McLoughlin,** an extinct volcano. At 9,495 feet, it's the dominant peak in Southern

Oregon, though not visible in Ashland because of the lower mountains surrounding it.

The lake, a county reservoir, is long and narrow, with enough space to allow water-skiing, some houseboats, and some sailboats.

Hyatt Lake

Staying on this road, continue to the next lake, **Hyatt Lake**, also a reservoir. It's smaller and has fewer activities, but still it's beautiful and worth a visit just to view or to picnic.

Lake of the Woods

Unlike the previous lakes, **Lake of the Woods** is not a reservoir. Again, conifers grow down to the water's edge, and its elevation is about a mile high. On the wall of the restaurant is a detailed map of the area, showing the trails that go up Mt. McLoughlin. There are roads to explore around the lake, some giving vistas of the lake, some of the mountain.

Four Mile Lake

Returning to the main road and continuing about one mile, you come to State Highway 140, which is where the route starts to circle back toward Medford. State 140 is wider and faster driving than Dead Indian Memorial Road, though still beautiful.

Four Mile Lake and Fish Lake are both off State 140. About one mile after turning on to

Hwy 140, you come to the **Four Mile Lake** turn-off on the right. The lake is listed as six miles in, and serves as the base for trails going up Mt. McLoughlin. It's reached by a gravel road (wash-board effect for part of it). As a result it's off the beaten track and sees fewer visitors. So it's not a surprise that it's rather rustic and feels more remote and quiet.

This is also a reservoir, and from the dam location we had lovely views of the back side of Mt. McLoughlin. Surrounding the lake are lovely conifers but also, curiously, countless fallen trees. Four Mile Lake is a quiet place popular for camping, fishing, and hiking. Boating is another attraction — there's a boat ramp — but all the boats we saw were non-motorized. There are pit toilets, and drinking water comes from a hand-powered pump. Fishermen, folks with non-powered boats, and campers enjoy this pretty lake.

Fish Lake

Fish Lake is right by the road near here and perhaps not as Alpine looking as the other lakes. It too is available for picnicking or camping, though there are neither stores nor restaurants. This spot caters to fishermen. Hiking trails start here, too. Elevation is 4,635 feet.

Willow Lake

A short distance beyond Fish Lake is the county road Rt. 821 heading for the town of Butte

Falls. Turn to the right, and after about 12 miles you'll arrive at **Willow Lake**. It lies at the foot of Mt. McLoughlin, so the views of the mountain are spectacular. The lake is also a little off the beaten track and makes you feel like you're more in the wilderness, with wild fauna and birds in evidence. You may fish and enjoy water sports. They have many of the same amenities offered at the other lakes — a marina (where you may rent various boats), a lounge, a small general store, and campgrounds.

Willow Lake is the last in this first group of lakes. For the next group, turn to the right and you're on your way to the next three lakes.

Lost Creek Reservoir, Crater Lake, and Diamond Lake

These next three lakes are on or near State Rt. 62 and are somewhat larger lakes than the ones admired on the Mountain Lakes Drive. After leaving Medford, **Lost Creek** is the first lake you come upon, and it's easy to just whiz by if you're on your way to Crater Lake. Sure, there's a lot of water over there, but it's somewhat masked by shrubbery. But slow down and enjoy the lovely occasional views. The lake is 10-miles long, and there are areas for picnicking and camping, as well as boating, fishing, and hiking.

Before you get to this body of water, you see signs to Cole Rivers Fish Hatchery, which is at the southwestern end of the lake. For more information about the hatchery see the chapter on *Medford,* (pp. 85). A visit to the hatchery allows you to wander around the various holding ponds in this largest of Oregon's hatcheries and see young fish in different stages of development. There is also a visitor center with restrooms and educational displays — both regarding fish and the local animal life. There's no charge for wandering around the tanks or for visiting this educational center.

Not far from the entrance to the hatchery and before reaching the lake is a small park with a visitor center manned by a ranger. This is a nice shady spot for a picnic and offers a lovely view of the Rogue River, which sweeps past the park.

Drive back to Route 62 and continue northeast. Almost immediately the road follows the lake's beautiful waterline. I haven't explored the facilities around Lost Creek Reservoir but this pleasant lake is obviously large enough to accommodate both boating and fishing interests. It's a perfect place to water ski because it's so long. The highway crosses the lake on a bridge (not the dam) toward the end of the lake, and the road continues the ascent into the mountains and forests.

Following the signs to Crater Lake you pass Prospect, a small town with interesting falls, which we'll visit in the chapter titled *Rivers and Waterfalls,* (pp. 179).

As signs indicate, the road to **Crater Lake** turns off to the right. Soon you arrive at this wonder. Its general history is that the volcano (Mount Mazama) literally blew its top during a violent prehistoric eruption. As years passed, the caldera filled with water that's very cold because of the nearly constant addition of melting snow.

To appreciate this lake, you need to do more than take a peek. The Visitor Center — a new and splendid building — is located near where the entrance road arrives at the lake. In front of the Center is a large parking lot with a broad viewing area beyond it. Stop and enjoy the view before proceeding.

A slow drive around the crater will pass occasional additional viewing spots. There are also several short trails that climb the rim and provide lovely views of the lake and its two islands — Wizard and Phantom Ship. About halfway around the lake there is a place where you can park and hike down to the water's edge to take a guided boat ride around the caldera. (A ranger is your guide, and tickets and schedules for rides on these boats are available at the Visitor Center.) An interesting but familiar oddity we found is that the trail of about one mile down, seems more like five on the return trip up. Could be that the elevation has something to do with it. But it's worth the effort if you're fit enough to do it. (Pamphlets advise visitors to not exceed their capacity. If this would be hard for you, enjoy the lake from the rim.)

You never know what you'll find along the way. We drove around the lake one sunny July day and were amazed to find a part of the road threading through perhaps 10-foot high banks of snow. It had been a long hard winter, and spring had not yet arrived here.

After you've enjoyed Crater Lake return to highway 62 and continue until it meets State Highway 230. (There are breathtaking things to see here, but we're talking about lakes now and we'll return to this spot in the Rivers and Falls chapter.) If you're out of time, turn to the left and retrace the road to Medford and then Ashland. If you have more time, turn to the right on Hwy 230 and follow the signs to Diamond Lake.

Enroute, you'll soon come to a large parking lot for viewing the outstanding countryside. It's on the right side of the road, and here are brass plaques explaining the history of Crater Lake. This stop is well worth the time.

Also at this location is the start of the **trail to the Boundary Springs**, the beginning of the Rogue River. If you take this trail, you have a nice hike partly through mosquito beds. I advise wearing long sleeves and long pants if you start here. This hike is described in more detail in the part about hikes found in the chapters named *Sports,* (pp. 136) and *Rivers and Waterfalls,* (pp. 181). (At Hamaker Campground, you can enter this trail much closer to the springs and skip the mosquitoes.)

Continuing on the highway, on the horizon above the intersection of highways 230 and 136 is a tall mountain with a very pointed peak, Mt. Thielsen. This is what's left of an ancient volcano. It overlooks **Diamond Lake**, so turn to the left, and a short distance along Highway 136 is the turnoff to the lake/resort.

Similar to vistas around Crater Lake there are many scenic views of sparkling Diamond Lake and surroundings. Since the water is a little warmer, swimming and boating are popular. A boat ramp is provided. You can also fish, hike, and camp here. (Camping is available for small or large groups both in tents and with trailers.) Picnicking is available for intimate family settings or for larger groups. Since this is a resort, most of what you get is very beautiful and nicely appointed.

After you've enjoyed your drive and walks around this lovely setting, retrace your steps back to Hwy 230 and Hwy 62. Then follow the signs to Medford and Ashland.

Lakes East of I-5

Applegate Lake

Applegate Lake is actually a large reservoir, and lies just about on the state line with California. To get there you drive through Jacksonville and keep going on Rt. 238, which goes directly to the dam and lake.

The two-lane road includes gentle turns through hilly country. We found the road lovely and a pleasure to drive. When you reach the dam, you can walk out on the structure to admire the sights. Or you can drive across the dam to the other side and drive along the water, even briefly crossing into California. Back at the main road, continue on to another road turning off to the left to take you down to Swayne's Point and closer to water's edge. There's a small store here with snacks and fishing supplies. There are also a few picnic tables dotting the area.

Applegate Lake offers a variety of water-related activities: swimming, boating — there are boat ramps — and fishing. There are also several hiking trails around the lake and up into the surrounding hills. Handicapped facilities are available, and public restrooms are provided. Overnight camping is available.

Lake Selmac

Lake Selmac is near Cave Junction on U.S. 199, just north of Kerby, about five minutes from Hwy. 199. There are clear signs directing you to the lake, a Josephine County Park, available for day use only.

Once at the lake we were impressed with its beauty and surprised to find that a lot of the surrounding grassy places were manicured, not just around the houses but in the general parklands, too. The mown lawns cry out to be sat upon, but we never saw anyone indulge in this pleasure.

One of several fields is for sports activities, but we didn't see children playing ball. On the two visits we made here, we didn't hear the ring of laughter of children at play. In all, the atmosphere is very quiet, calm, and serene.

There are picnic tables, camping places, a boat ramp, and a dock. This is an area mostly for fishing and boating. According to a local gentleman, there is a small area — around the dock — for swimming.

One final possible activity is horseback riding. There is an old sign directing to a riding stable, but we never saw the stables. Like several other sites we've visited in Southern Oregon, there are monuments to war heroes or events

We saw no entrance booth for collecting fees at the lake, and our conversation with a mature workman about what activities were available included no comment about paying such a fee. This may be taken care of in the small store there, but, again, we saw no signs with that requirement.

You can also enjoy visiting Lake Semac Resort where you can rent cabins year around, rent a boat, picnic, play mini-golf, fish, swim, ride horses, etc. Phone 541-597-2277 or check on-line www.lakeselmac.com.

Our first trip to Lake Selmac followed a trip to the caves, and there wasn't enough time to enjoy the area, but our second visit included plans to picnic before the cave trip. We found our spot, and after looking around were delighted to find wild berries — ripe for eating — edging one side of the picnic area. We picked a handful of berries — leaving lots for the next visitors — washed them at a nearby faucet, and thoroughly enjoyed them. Ah, serendipity!

There were restrooms, which looked primitive, but since this is a camping place also, they're probably acceptable. Since we were on our way to the caves, which we knew to have fine restrooms, we didn't visit and investigate these.

Now that we've explored lakes, we'll explore rivers/waterfalls and other water-oriented locations, some quite spectacular, in the next chapter.

Rivers and Waterfalls

Rivers

Note: Since there's not much variety in what you can say about rivers in the context of what to do, I'm basically just going to list them and tell where they are. All the listed rivers (but not Lithia Creek) have recreational possibilities from wading and swimming to fishing and boating.

Rivers and creeks are plentiful in Southern Oregon and Northern California. The closest is **Lithia Creek** in Lithia Park, Ashland. It has water 12 months of the year, so you can always get your feet wet here (though I've never seen anyone fish).

Farther away, it is possible to visit the starting places, the sources, of two significant rivers in the area covered in this book. In the chapter titled *Sports*, (pp. 131), there's a section focusing on hikes, and one of these hikes is to The Boundary Springs, the source for the Rogue River. The other starting place (also a spring) is for the Sacramento River, in Northern California at Mt. Shasta city. Think of it, in about one step you can cross over the very beginnings of these two great rivers.

In considering rivers in the area, let's start with the **Rogue River**, which runs from Crater Lake to the ocean (just north of Gold Beach). There are many places to swim or wade in this stream, but some of the spots easily reached from Ashland are: 1) at Evans Perry Park in the city of Rogue River, 2) at the rest stop along I-5, called Valley of the Rogue State Park, 3) at Grants Pass city parks, and 4) along Hwy 62 near Shady Cove.

There are three places along the Rogue that deserve special attention: **Boundary Springs** (referred to above), **Rogue Gorge**, and **Natural Bridges**. Visiting Boundary Springs involves a significant but not difficult hike, and additional information is to be found in the Hikes part of the chapter named *Sports*, (pp. 131).

Boundary Springs

Directions: Take I-5 to Medford and Hwy 62 to Crater Lake. Union Creek is just before the turnoff to Crater Lake. Switch to Hwy 230 and drive another few miles to the large parking lot on the right — Crater Rim Viewpoint — to learn about the ancient Mt. Mazama Volcano.

Boundary Springs is the source of the Rogue River and springs out near the sides of the caldera, which forms Crater Lake. The water starts small, benign, and narrow — you can cross the stream on a simple log bridge — and soon becomes a wide and impressive river. There are two ways to reach the Springs. One is to drive to Union City and take the left fork in the road, Rt. 230, rather than staying on Hwy 62 which takes you into Crater Lake territory. Proceed on Hwy 230 to a large pullout area with parking, called Crater Rim Viewpoint. Enjoy the bronze tablets giving information about the geographic history and the beginning and development of Crater Lake.

To get to the Springs, you proceed from this point on foot. (The hike is not strenuous but it is a hike and you need sturdy shoes, not summer sandals.) When we hiked this trail we found that it wasn't well marked at the top. Someone had apparently removed one or more signs pointing the way. (When we told the rangers on the trip back to town, they said they'd check it out; so very likely all signs are in place now.) Once we were on the trail, the route was clear.

This is correctly described as an "easy-to-moderate difficulty" trail. Due to a nasty encounter with mosquitoes, we didn't take the whole walk the first time around — only about 1.5 miles of an about five-mile round trip. For our next attempt, we wore long pants and shirts covering our legs and arms (plus a spritz of insect repellent), and we were protected from these pests. On this first attempt, we got as far as the place where the trail crosses the Rogue River on eight-foot-long logs, making the river just a few feet wide and quite tame at this point, and our interest was definitely roused. So, a year later, when we came back prepared for the worst, we were enchanted with the beauty of the area and enjoyed the whole walk.

You wander among ferns and Lodge Pole Pine trees. While the hilly trail is basically uphill on the return trip, it's not very steep.

After we had completed the walk we found that there's another shorter, easier way to get to the Springs. On Hwy 62 in the Rogue River National Forest, before you reach the Rim

Viewpoint, look for signs to Hamaker Camp Grounds. Following the dirt road, it eventually gets to a parking place where you can leave your car and walk the rest of the way to the Springs. Taking this route you cut the distance about in half, still enjoying ferns and trees. Either way, it's a hike well worth the effort.

On both hikes we returned to the Crater Rim Viewpoint where we enjoyed the view and the descriptive plaques. On our first trip we were there when the snow from a late storm was still in evidence on the rim, making it clearly different from the surrounding hills and forest. The explanatory plaques have drawings explaining the vista, in addition to information describing the catastrophic eruption of Mt. Mazama that eventually resulted in Crater Lake.

Rogue Gorge and Natural Bridges occur a few miles away from the Springs, after the river has become a significant stream. In these two related areas the river tears through a rock-lined canyon with amazing results.

Rogue Gorge

To get there from Medford, take Hwy 62 to Union City, near the turnoff to Crater Lake. In Union City, a big sign about this attraction directs you to the parking lot right by the highway.

To see the Gorge, you have to take an easy foot trail — paved, quite short, quite level, and quite spectacular! This is at least a four-star stop!

The clearly marked trail with interesting interpretive signs leads you past one breathtaking view after another of the turbulent waters, the mighty surge and thunder as the water bursts through the narrow canyon.

This is a wow trail, and since it's so short, we take it every time we're in the area!

Natural Bridges

The next stop is a sister attraction and is a scant five minutes closer to Medford at the Natural Bridges viewpoint and campgrounds. There's a sign to Natural Bridges, which directs cars to pass along the campground road. Take the one way "Y" in the road to the parking lot, and then proceed on a slightly longer footpath than the one to the Gorge. This one is also well paved and easy. A footbridge crosses the Rogue River after it's passed through the canyon. Standing on the bridge and looking upstream you get a quick overview of the area.

The name "Natural Bridge" brings to my memory pictures of other natural bridges I've visited — majestic arches carved out by wind or waves. Some were quiet places in the desert; others were formed by crashing waves at the ocean. This is quite different from either. This "bridge" should actually be "bridges" and might more accurately be called tubes, because it's where the Rogue River has invaded old lava tubes. The river flows underground for a short distance and then explodes out into the open again. The whole thing takes place in a narrow rock-lined canyon, which restricts and intensifies the flow of the water, resulting in the water taking great pounding leaps over boulders and around bends. The trail is far enough above the water on both trails that you don't get a drop of moisture on you.

If you do nothing else in the area, take these two trails. Being in a wheelchair or on crutches is no impediment to going, for we saw people in both situations on both trails. So, if need be, get someone to push your chair or you take your time with the crutches. There are a few places to sit down along the path — so go. You'll be glad you did.

Back to Simply Rivers

Applegate River, a part of the Rogue River system, is far more serene. It runs gently through meadows and under trees before emptying into the Applegate Lake/reservoir on the California/Oregon state line. At McKee Covered Bridge or nearby Cantrall-Buckley County Park are wonderful places to wade or swim in the Applegate.

In the Cave Junction area is the **Illinois River** flowing past the Illinois River State Park. If you're patient, you may see some turtles sunning themselves on the banks in the park. The Illinois River eventually runs into the Rogue River before it empties into the ocean.

Closer to the ocean, mostly in California, but still on Hwy 199 is the **Smith River**. Hwy 199 crosses and re-crosses this clear, beautiful stream as it wanders among and over rocks and boulders and through conifers and other trees and shrubs. Most of the road stays above the river, but it sometimes gets close enough to it that getting your feet wet is quite easy. The highway designers provided several viewing places/parking lots where you can either take pictures — which you will want to do — or get out and splash in the water. It looks as if the river is neither calm enough nor deep enough for swimming.

The **Umpqua River** is north of both the Rogue River and Crater Lake, and together with creeks that flow into it, is the source for the falls described later in this chapter. See *Waterfall Drive,* (pp. 195). The Umpqua continues north and west until it empties into the Pacific near Reedsport, north of Coos Bay.

In Northern California, you'll find the **Klamath River** near the state line, bordering the beautiful first rest stop as you drive south on I-5, and of course the **Sacramento River** south of Mt. Shasta city. I-5 crisscrosses the Sacramento as you drive south.

I'll not list other lovely rivers and streams because there are so many. But if you look while you're out driving, you'll have the opportunity to see many others, some with interesting names. Perhaps you'll find a favorite.

Waterfalls

If the sight of a lovely waterfall interests you, or the sound soothes you, you'll have several opportunities to be interested or soothed in Southern Oregon and Northern California. We'll visit three near Crater Lake. Further north there's a drive you can take that follows along a river — the Umpqua — that produces many falls. Then there are communities like Butte Falls and Klamath Falls that have one, of which they're rather proud. While I wouldn't try to visit all of them in one day, this chapter will visit several of the falls in a sort of geographical order, starting in two communities in Oregon.

Butte Falls

Directions: To get there, start in Medford and take Hwy 62 toward Crater Lake. Before the highway rises into the hills, just beyond Eagle Point, is the road eastward to Butte Falls.

This is a pleasant two-lane road through agricultural or ranching interests in rolling hills. When you reach **Butte Falls** you won't find signs to the falls without looking for them. First, go ahead to the center of town to a large square park. At the near corner is a statue of Ralph Bunyan, Paul Bunyan's little brother. Ralph was apparently of normal size, and was remarkable only for being the brother of a celebrity. The statue is behind chain-link protection.

To get to the falls, retrace the route you took into town and look for the sign on your right that leads to a recycling business and the falls. The road soon becomes a gravel and then dirt track, but don't give up. Soon you arrive at a flat, cleared area with ruins of a now forgotten building. There was once a mill here, but these ruins could at best be only a part of what was once an important part of this old logging town. Park here. You'll hear the sound of the falls and see a wooden landing for viewing them. At certain times of the year the area is fairly covered with wild flowers.

The falls are low (perhaps eight feet high) and cover the whole width of Big Butte Creek, making an impressive sight. I believe there is also a picnic table. Take a few pictures, eat a snack, enjoy nature's offering, then pack up your things and drive back to Hwy 62. This would be considered a nice, lazy afternoon outing. It's something you could do with a handicapped person.

Klamath Falls

Directions: This waterfall, which has the same name as the city, is at the south end of Klamath Lake, the largest fresh water lake in the state. To get there, the fastest route again is to start from Medford on Hwy 62 and turn right on Hwy 140 going east, which eventually gets you into Klamath Falls.

This town is larger than Butte Falls and has a bit more going for it. In fact, the falls almost take a backseat to these other places of interest. For instance, in addition to the falls, and near them, there are three museums featuring local and regional history, including a display of Indian artifacts. Check with these museums for their hours and fees. All are located on Main Street. The names and phone numbers are: Favell Museum, which is probably the largest (541-882-9996); Klamath County Museum (541-883-4208); and the old Baldwin Hotel Museum with its display, including original furnishings from the early 1900's (541-883-4207). These venues are available at a variety of times, and all charge an entrance fee.

There's also a self-guiding walking tour not associated with the museums. Check with the local Information Center for amount of fees and get maps.

Surrounding the town are six wildlife refuges, including Lower Klamath National Wildlife Refuge, established by President Theodore Roosevelt in 1908, now the oldest waterfowl refuge in the USA. Tule Lake, listed in other parts of this book, (see chapter on *Northern California,* pp. 264) is one of these wildlife refuges.

Finally, Klamath Falls has an interesting phenomenon — an underground supply of geothermal-heated water. This water is used to heat a variety of structures (homes, schools, and business) and to melt snow from their sidewalks.

When you have finished your visit here, retrace your steps along Hwy 140 to Hwy 62.

You're now near Medford. To visit more falls, turn to the right. To go back to Ashland, turn left and follow the directional signs.

The Drive from Medford to Union Creek

If you wish to skip the two above-mentioned communities with their museums, etc., start here with the next section, dedicated more to nature and falls, taking Hwy 62 out of Medford. This part of the road is the same route you take to get to Crater Lake and Boundary Springs. On the way, enjoy the sights. You pass through Shady Cove where it's possible to rent rafts for use on their river, the Rogue. There are free shuttles to the river. Trail rides and hikes also originate in Shady Cove.

There's an inviting-looking campground with day use and picnic tables just beyond town, riverside. A few miles beyond this campground is another (Casey State Park) also very clean and attractive. Both are long and narrow, with as much riverfront as possible. A little further along on the other side of the highway (just before the Lost Creek Reservoir) is The Cole Rivers Fish Hatchery and visitor center.

The road soon wanders beside beautiful Lost Creek Reservoir and passes Stewart State Park, which offers picnicking, camping, a restaurant, a marina, and a boat ramp. Then Hwy 62 crosses the far end of the lake on a large bridge, not the dam. When the highway starts to ascend into the hills, you are driving through Rogue River National Forest.

Farther along Hwy 62, just after the town of Prospect, (which we'll visit on the way back), is the ranger station on the left. Here the friendly personnel will provide maps and information about local trails and falls, including directions to Boundary Springs. They also have picnic tables and maintain clean restrooms.

Once inside the National Forest you'll see a number of picnicking or camping areas sprinkled along the way — most if not all provide pit toilets. We saw no restaurants except in the towns.

In most of the rest of this chapter, there will be ample opportunities to hike some trails. None of them are difficult, but proper footwear would be helpful. I don't necessarily recommend wearing hiking boots, but I do think regular shoes (including tennies) are a good idea and much preferred to flip-flops or high heels. These preferred shoes will enable you to stride out on the sometimes uneven surface of the trails. (Unbelievably, I have seen a few ladies trying to hike in heels.)

There are many lovely falls in this area, and I'm going to start with the one farthest away and work my way back.

Waterfalls and Other Water Wonders Near Crater Lake

National Creek Falls

Directions: Take Hwy 62 to Union Creek. From Union Creek, continue on Hwy 62 for approximately six more miles and turn to the right on Forest Road #6530, the turn off to the falls. Proceed 3.85 miles to the trailhead.

A picture of National Creek Falls hangs on the wall of one of the ranger stations, and its beauty encouraged us to trace down the falls for a visit. We were told that to reach it one takes a short, easy trail (.4 miles in length). Good. It was not only beautiful but could be reached by taking a short, easy hike. The rangers told us to follow Hwy 62 nearly six miles beyond Union Creek and look for the signs on the right side of the highway. That sounded easy, too. However, nearly all the directional signs were missing, so we took a few wrong turns before we found the right road and the parking area near the top of the falls. We reached it by what has become an explorer's "seat-of-the-pants" rule — if it doesn't look right, it probably isn't! One hint: once off the highway, skip the first turn and keep going a bit more.

Finally at the parking area we headed out on foot. The trail is direct — pretty much zigzagging straight down (and later straight up) but it was worth it. We hiked on a warm day, and upon reaching the falls we were met with a fine, refreshing cool mist from the water splashing off boulders. The fall was indeed beautiful, and we looked at it from as many perspectives as the base-of-the-falls landing would permit. A fallen tree made getting very close difficult, but leaning out a bit gave us good views from which to photograph the scene.

This is not a picnic area, simply a viewing opportunity. Would I visit again? Absolutely!

Once you've enjoyed National Creek Falls, return to Hwy 62 and turn to the left, toward Prospect. Along the way the road passes the aforementioned Boundary Spring Trail, and the spectacular Rogue Gorge and Natural Bridges. If you haven't visited these last places, be sure to now. Or if you enjoyed them as much as I do, visit them again. The hikes are quite short and the beauty is outstanding. Then drive on to Prospect.

Mill Creek and Barr Creek Falls

There are two waterfalls in the Prospect area — Mill Creek and Barr Creek. Both would be pleasant, hot day activities, for the path roams through forested land, a few degrees cooler than the open area. Wheelchairs couldn't make this trip.

Mill Creek Falls and **Barr Creek Falls** are viewed after taking a short, easy hike through Boise-Cascade land. To get to the start of this trail, drive about two miles off Hwy 62 on Mill

Creek Road to the small town of Prospect. (This road looks like it is the old highway.)

Signs along the road point to the location of the falls and its parking lot, so watch for them on the left as you drive south. The woodsy trail is .3-miles long, unpaved, wide, and moderately downhill to a viewing spot of the falls, both of which drop from the cliff across the Rogue River.

The two falls are near each other. The first is Mill Creek Falls itself, which drops 173 feet. Continuing a short distance along the trail you come to the second, Barr Creek Falls, which drops a similar distance and is seen through a rainbow mist. Go a few feet beyond this second spot to stand on the rocks, and you get a different view. (Be careful of your footing because there are no handrails.) You'll see hidden behind a tree a second wispy fall to the left of the main fall. So, Barr Creek Falls is actually two.

Boise-Cascade has sunk markers along the trail identifying different plants. They've done a nice job of it.

The shady path was welcome on the warm afternoon, but it might be slippery on a rainy day, for the surface is compacted dirt. This was a short, pleasant trip.

When hiking back to the car, if you're surefooted and feeling adventurous, take the right fork in the trail, which leads down to river's edge. It takes you through "Avenue of Boulders," a field of huge boulders, sometimes even over smaller ones. We found that this detour was not overly strenuous, and the accompanying spray from the river was very welcome on the hot day. This walk certainly isn't for everyone, but judging from the well-worn look, it apparently sees a lot of traffic. If you can manage the uncertain footing, this is a cool and refreshing diversion. Otherwise, take the left fork to return to your car.

Waterfall Drive

There is a drive, which takes you past a series of several waterfalls along the Umpqua River.

Directions: To start this drive, take Hwy 62 from Medford past the Crater Lake exit, until Hwy 62 dead-ends at Hwy 230. Turn to the right and drive to Hwy 138. Then turn to the left, continuing past Diamond Lake. From here nearly to Roseburg is one majestic fall after another. None are viewable from the highway, and some involve a significant hike. All have parking and identifying signs, easily read from the road.

To help you decide which falls to investigate, visit the ranger station as you pass Prospect to get a complete map/brochure, which includes additional information, such as distances and degree of difficulty. With this map you can make choices according to your time and capabilities.

I'm going to list a few of the trails we either hiked or considered hiking and skipped for lack of time. But first, a few general comments: Probably none of these trails would be suitable for wheelchairs, though one stop has the fall viewable from the parking lot. Another trail involves climbing a rather long flight of metal stairs. Some of the trails are described as taking several hours to complete, and I don't list them. You'll need the complete detailed map to help you here. In all cases there are clear signs along the highway identifying each fall.

Here are some of the shorter hikes.

1. Susan Creek Falls – 0.8 miles to a fall with a 50-foot drop.
2. Fall Creek Falls – one mile through lush forest and along the river, with one segment through a narrow rock crevice. Part of the trail is a little steep. The fall is double-tiered. Families enjoy this one.
3. Medicine Creek pictographs – 1.3 miles to this 8,000-year-old religious site. "This site is very fragile and is protected by law; please treat it with respect," says the pamphlet.
4. Toketee Falls – 0.4 mile over a trail that includes 200 steps leading to an observation platform. The fall is double-tiered and spectacular. There are interpretive panels.
5. Watson Falls – just over one mile round trip. With a 293 feet drop, this is the highest waterfall in southwest Oregon.
6. Whitehorse Falls – This is the one that has a viewing platform near the parking area, and

the fall is viewable from the car. The falls drop into a "punchbowl" pool.

7. Clearwater Falls is reached after a "short walk." These falls are a cascade tumbling over mossy rocks.

Two of us hiked about three of the trails at an easy pace and arrived in Roseburg in time for dinner. Since we took no other walks or stops other than for a picnic and pit stop, this would be an all-day outing, not difficult but highly satisfying. After dinner we returned south on I-5 to Ashland at a time too late to take in a play.

In Northern California

Dunsmuir and Mt. Shasta city

Both cities have inviting downtown areas, providing a good balance of hotels/motels and eating establishments. Both also have about every public service business you'd need – banks, gas stations, etc. Both have lovely falls, but we couldn't visit all of them in the time we had. Dunsmuir has two: Mossbrae Falls and Hedge Creek Falls. To visit the Dunsmuir falls named **Hedge Creek Falls**, exit I-5 at Hwy 732 (North Dunsmuir Avenue). There's an immediate sharp right turn, almost a U-turn, at the end of the exit road. Here you can park on dirt and gravel by the side of the road. Follow signs to the trailhead. The trail takes a fork and you want the one more traveled, the one to the left. This trail is an easy switchback, leading down to the falls. Once there you notice that the path leads behind the falls, providing instant air conditioning, but not getting you too wet. If you have come only to view the falls, stay a few minutes to enjoy, take a few pictures, and then head back the way you came. Otherwise, you could keep going and explore the trail, which continues further on the other side of the falls before you eventually return to your car. When back at the top, notice the beautiful views of Mt. Shasta peeking through the trees.

For a lovely added stop in Dunsmuir, stay on North Dunsmuir Road and follow the signs to their city park, a small botanical garden, where you'll find a picnic area, the gardens, tennis courts, and playing fields.

Adjacent to the gardens are public restrooms.

Now proceed to Mt. Shasta city. To get there return to I-5 for the short drive to exit 738. Turn left on North Mt. Shasta Blvd. and left again on Dixon. Follow the signs through the parking area to the **headwaters of the Sacramento River.** Yes, the Headwaters are actually springs, but let's not get too technical. Details of our visit here are in the chapter on *Northern California,* (pp. 251).

After you enjoy this lovely area, you can now either return to Ashland or progress to the Shasta Lake and Redding areas for more adventures.

Peaks and Mesas

This chapter is included in part to answer that not infrequent ponder, "I wonder what mountain that is?" But before getting into names, what's the difference between a peak, a mesa, and a rock — all mentioned in this chapter and elsewhere in this book? "Peak" refers to those parts of the surrounding land that stand above the rest, often having a pointed top. A "mesa" also stands out from the surrounding countryside, but it has rather vertical sides and a flat top. A "rock" again stands out from its surroundings, but is a large mass of rock jutting up. Most of the peaks are extinct or dormant volcanoes. Not to get too technical about it, the rocks I mention are volcanic plugs.

Let me define two further vocabulary words just mentioned — dormant and extinct. Dormant means a volcano hasn't erupted for a while but may in the next hundred years or so, for it's only sleeping. Extinct means that it hasn't erupted in recorded time and isn't expected to do so again.

Mt. Ashland

Mt. Ashland is not a volcano, but a high point in the Coast Range, which is also in California. (The Coast Range is caused by uplift, not volcanic activity.) The mountain is 7,500 feet tall, which is not the highest peak in Southern Oregon, but it's the most visible from the city of Ashland and I-5.

Skiing is popular here in the winter partly because of its easy access and also its close proximity to housing. There are picnic tables for warmer weather. We made the trip to the top one February and found many skiers enjoying the slopes. Later, when we visited in the summer, the elevated region was cooler than the valley and a welcome respite from its heat, but there were few visitors. Perhaps they were busy with other activities, or perhaps they thought Mt. Ashland could be enjoyed only in the winter. If you make this trip in August, you might find you have the whole area to yourself, but would be nicely cool.

Mt. Ashland is also the beginning (or ending) of a beautiful but challenging drive from the Ruch area. It's an unpaved logging road with breathtaking views of the region, such as clear views of Mt. Shasta in Northern California. But this is not a road for the faint of heart, and vehicles with high clearance are recommended by the rangers. Identifying it as a logging road should give you a clue as to the type of road it is, and there has been no effort to make the drive easy. It's bumpy and windy. There are no signs identifying the main road from the shorter offshoots used by the big trucks. Happily, on the few times we've traversed this road we met no logging truck. The fact that we repeated the drive for a total of three trips says something either about our courage or foolishness, or (more accurately) the absolute beauty of the views. The road has a name — Siskiyou Loop Drive — and I might drive it again, but if you're a timid driver or have an undependable car ... well, there are other things to do!

You could probably find hiking trails up here, but I haven't explored them. The nearest ranger station (in Ashland) can answer that question and provide you with appropriate maps, including one for the Siskiyou Loop Drive.

Pilot Rock

Here's an example of a rock. It stands out on the horizon, being visible for miles as you drive I-5 to the Ashland area from California. It's easy to see why early pioneers gave it this name and used it as a navigational guide. They could clearly see it and knew that they were approaching the Rogue River valley. When we see it, we know we're about to enter Oregon.

Mt. Shasta

This dormant volcano is in Northern California. It's not visible from Ashland, but on your trip south it comes into sight as you wind around I-5 about the time you cross into California. I've made this trip many times, and sometimes the weather is such that Mt. Shasta is hidden in part or wholly by clouds, even as I drive through scorching heat. It apparently creates its own weather.

Table Rock Mountains

Directions: Exit I-5 at the last Medford exit (exit 33). Take Hwy. 99 north of Medford to Table Rock Road and turn to the right. This road crosses over I-5, and then proceeds until you're at the mesas.

Clearly visible from I-5, to the right as you head north from Medford, is a large mesa. When we were early in the area, we inquired about it, drove around a bit, and found that there are two mesas near each other, reminding me of the better-known "Mittens" of Monument Valley, Arizona, though quite unlike them in shape. For more details of the Table Rocks, read under Hikes in *Sports,* (pp. 134).

Mt. McLoughlin

Mt. McLoughlin is a part of the Cascade Range with its many peaks, such as the Three Sisters near Bend in Eastern Oregon. You can't see this lovely extinct volcano from Ashland because there are low hills blocking your view. As you drive north from Ashland, you get to a position near Medford where you can see Mt. McLoughlin, standing by itself in all its glory. It has the highest elevation in Southern Oregon, and by the time you near The Table Rock Mountains, your perspective has changed, so you see wonderful views of the peak.

There are hiking trails here, but they're recommended only for the more experienced hiker due to the strenuous ascent and descent. Read the section about hiking in the chapter on *Sports,* (pp. 131), before you attempt this. According to those who have hiked the mountain, it would not be an easy outing and may take more effort than you want.

Mt. Thielsen

This extinct volcano keeps watch over Diamond Lake (near the intersection of Highways 230 and 138). It has a distinctive shape, a very pointed peak, easily distinguished on the horizon and in photographs. Its jagged peak is the result of centuries of erosion. Mt. Thielsen has been hit so many times by lightning that it has earned the name of Lightning Rod of the Cascades, and there are rocks on the peak showing fusion related to lightning strikes.

There are hiking trails here and at nearby Diamond Lake.

Rabbit Ears

Once you've seen this volcanic plug you'll understand why it's so named. Twin-shaped plugs can be seen west of Hwy 230 near Mt. Thielsen. This pair of promontories is popular with climbers.

As you look at the skyline around Ashland, you see many additional mountains, but I don't know their names. They appear to be more a part of a range of mountains than being an outstanding peak, like these already named.

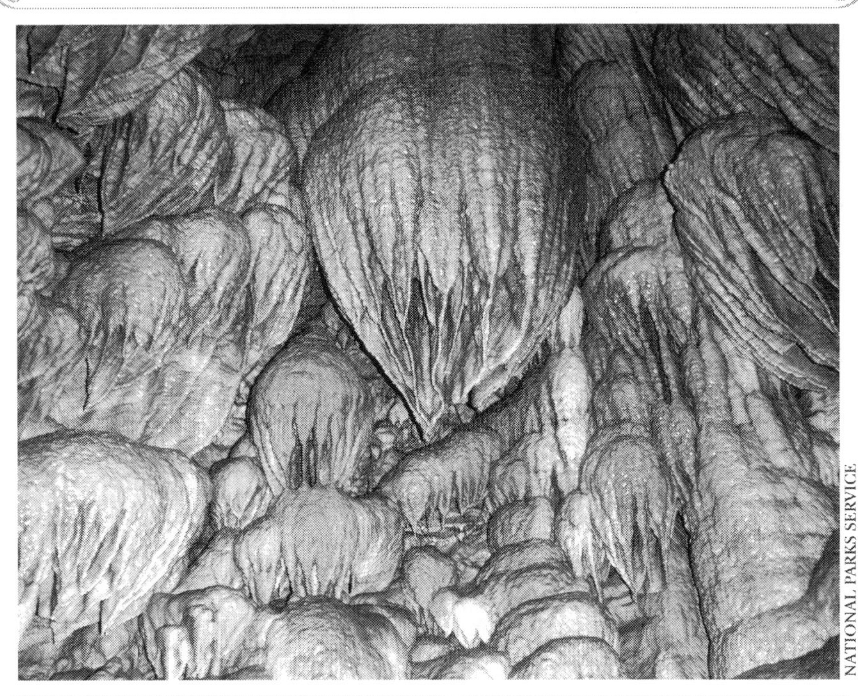
NATIONAL PARKS SERVICE

Caves

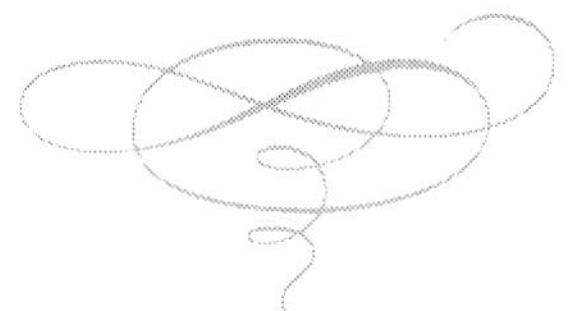

Oregon Caves National Monument

Directions: Take I-5 to Grants Pass, (about 40 minutes from Ashland) exit 55, then Rt. 199 south to Cave Junction. Turn east on Rt. 46. Each highway is narrower than the former, but all are quite acceptable roadways. Rt. 46, partly in the Siskiyou National Forest and mountains, is a slow mountain road of great beauty.

This whole drive is through scenic lands. One sign that amused this Californian was the one just after turning on to Rt. 199: "Redwood Empire, Cave Junction, and the Golden Gate Bridge." Since the latter is several hundred miles south, were the highway sign people making a little joke? Rt. 199 is a part of the Redwood Highway here, and eventually joins up with Rt. 101, California's Redwood Highway, which does indeed cross the Golden Gate Bridge; but it's at least a day's drive away with many interesting points in between.

As you drive toward Cave Junction, Rt. 199 crosses Applegate River, the same river that is near Jacksonville. Then the road passes Wilderville, which has signs mentioning a fish hatchery. (On one trip we turned off to investigate the hatchery and found that, contrary to the signs, the hatchery no longer exists.) Farther along Hwy 199, the road passes Kerby, which has a museum discussed in the chapter on *Museums,* (pp. 63). We stopped at this small, interesting collection of memorabilia largely because a ranger at the caves said it was worth a stop. She was right.

The roads are well marked, but you can't tell at first if the information posted on signs by the road is important to you. Some were indicating hiking trails, for instance. But to read the signs you have to slow down because some of them are small, green metal markers parallel to the road — more like city street signs than highway markers. You don't have to read these signs, but some of the names, dating from early mining days, are interesting.

Once at Cave Junction, you drive to the far end of town to the stop light with signs to The Oregon Caves. A glance around the town shows an active community with many well-known businesses. There's a sign which says the population is 1,200, but the businesses lead one to expect a larger population, so they obviously provide services for not only their residents but for the surrounding countryside as well. From this point follow the signs to the caves.

The six-mile drive from Cave Junction to the parking lot of the National Monument is especially scenic, climbing and twisting through forests of Douglas fir, rhododendrons, dogwood, madrone, myrtle, oak, and ferns; over and beside a rushing pure creek; and past a campground. Much of this has posted speed restrictions saying 20 miles per hour, due to the curves and scenery. So, take your time and enjoy.

(On one trip here, we arrived at Oregon Caves about 2:30 p.m. This included a few side stops. But even arriving fairly late in the day, we were still in time to take a tour through the caves. And by the way, this is another venue where you don't wander on your own but always go with a guide.)

The Oregon Caves parking lot is large and was rather crowded, which surprised us because we saw few cars on the road. The lot is new — a short walk from the visitor center and entrance to the caves. It was a hot day (with the temperature over 90 degrees), but we knew the caves were cold (**a steady 46 degrees** year round), so we changed into warmer clothes: long pants and shirts, real shoes instead of sandals, and carried jackets. (Once in the caves we were very glad for this foresight. Several people in our group who were dressed for 90 degrees were shivering.)

The road from the parking lot to the visitor center is short, paved, and rather wide since it doubles for the road to the chalet lodge near the ticket booth and is not a part of the National Monument. A wheelchair could easily take this part of the trip, but the caves are passable only by someone who walks comfortably. There are long flights of metal stairs to climb, for instance. Young children are not admitted, but childcare is provided for a fee. Mothers are not allowed to carry small children because the trail is fairly long and narrow, and the atmosphere is damp, so the metal stairs are potentially slippery. National Monument people have found from experience that carrying a small child could be tiring if not dangerous. There is a small set of steps by the ticket booth, intended mainly as a test for children. But if you have questions about your own ability to navigate the caves, try these steps, and if you find them challenging you're advised (by the rangers) not to take the trip.

Once you've bought your ticket, you join other visitors waiting for the next tour to be called, which typically consists of a group of about 20 people. Benches are provided outside the Caves entrance. Or one can stroll around the area, including the gift shop, being careful to not go beyond hearing distance.

When your tour is called, the visitors gather around the uniformed guides who are a part of the National Park Service. They have a sort of "memorized script" to share as you walk leisurely along, but they freely digress to answer questions or to point out something unusual — perhaps a sleeping bat. The trail is not difficult for the average ambulatory person. The guides do request that you not touch the walls, to balance yourselves or for any other reason, because the oil on your hands damages the cave walls.

Before you embark on the walk, consider how the caves were discovered. It was in 1874 when Elijah J. Davidson followed a bear he'd been tracking into one of the many cave openings in the area. He was alone, except for his dog, his rifle, and some matches. Apparently he never found the bear, but instead he found this astounding display of marble "rooms" filled with columns and pillars and connected with passageways sometimes too narrow to navigate. His matches could only suggest the colors and intricacies of the columns.

Today there are asphalt paths, steel steps, and an electric lighting system for illuminating this wonder. Each room has its own circuit of lights which is designed to be turned on by the ranger as the tour enters the room, and is turned off upon exiting it. The one-way trail leads slowly up through many individually lighted rooms of different sizes and on different levels. All along the way you see moisture continuing its job of creating stalactites and stalagmites. Only in a few places is the moisture enough to get you a bit damp. The formations are of different muted tones and a variety of shapes, some of them with names.

The intent of the Park Service is to preserve the caves. There is one stretch where early cave caretakers — unfortunately not well enlightened — blasted through some boulders to create the trail and then packed the debris into handy crevices, thereby filling in and covering portions of this natural wonder. The Park Service has recently worked at removing the debris as carefully as archeologists — with small brushes, trowels, and buckets.

Our guide had us make frequent stops to enjoy what we were passing. By the way, there is one place near the beginning of the tour where you can make an early exit if you want to, but we found it not too strenuous, very beautiful and interesting, and well worth whatever effort it took to see the whole tour.

At the end of the trail, you exit into the warm outside atmosphere, and there are benches where you can sit down and rest or remove unwanted extra clothes. Or you can just marvel at the different wonders — the lovely vista of forested lands.

From here you have two choices of trails back to the parking lot. The first is quite direct — the asphalt trail. The other is a nature trail that takes you a little farther up the mountain and through the trees to a wider vista of miles of forested mountains. Along the trail are signs labeling various plants or intriguing things of nature. This nature trail is less than a mile long and soon joins the other down trail and returns you to the ticket booth/visitor center. Here you can buy snacks including ice cream cones, which we found rather meager but cool and very welcome.

This trip to the caves is very different from anything else in Southern Oregon, and it's both interesting and beautiful. It's heartily recommended! However you feel about walking, if you can manage it, don't miss this wonderful place.

The tour took about 1 ½ hours, and the drive without interruption took about the same time. There are other interesting things to do in the area, such as the Great Cats World Park on Hwy 199 just beyond the Cave Junction (and discussed in the chapter on *Animals*, pp. 115) and the Kerbyville Museum (discussed in the chapter on *Museums*, pp. 63). But if you're interested in visiting only the caves, the return trip is just the reverse of the trip to the caves.

When you reach Grants Pass, you have two choices for your continued route. You can turn right and go through city traffic to the clearly marked route to I-5, passing those famous big-box stores, or you can take the scenic but much slower drive on Rt. 99. This follows the Rogue River. The route is 45 miles an hour, passing many congested areas. At the city of Rogue River you can get back to I-5.

Lava Beds National Monument

Directions: To get to the Lava Beds, leaving Ashland, take Oregon State Highway 66 east to Klamath Falls. Head south on State 39. Near Merrill the highway changes to California State 139. This road takes you past Tule Lake (discussed in the chapter on *Northern California – Central*, pp. 265) before arriving at nearby Lava Beds National Monument. There are signs along the way to either Tule Lake or the Lava Beds, clearly marking the route.

This Monument is in Northern California perhaps 10 miles from the California State line, and southeast of Klamath Falls. The Lava Beds were formed by eruptions from nearby Medicine Lake volcano. The Monument is in the heart of ancient lava beds, not far from mounts Shasta and Lassen. Neither has erupted appreciably for many, many years, but this area is covered with rocks and boulders from earlier eruptions.

One of the phenomena of lava eruptions is that they sometimes form what geologists call lava tubes. In this case they're areas underground where molten lava continued to flow through parts that had solidified on the outside, forming large roundish tubes when the eruption was finished. Now, years later, it is possible to walk through some of these cave-like areas and witness underground beauty. Some are too low for people to stand upright, and one would have to crawl or shimmy through them. But near the Visitor Center, there are guided tours through one of the larger tubes.

Worldwide, most caves that are open to the public have restrictions as to when and where you can wander, and this Monument is no exception. Some of the underground trails are bordered with red lights, and the staff provides flashlights for visitors to borrow — once they've paid and are on a waiting list for a tour. (These flashlights are especially useful when entering other caves not having lighting systems.) Feel free to bring your own lamps or flashlights.

The guided tour starts above ground where the guide introduces you to the geology of the area. Soon the tour takes the trail that descends down steep steps before leading into the darkness. In the cave we visited, there was a large area with folding chairs to accommodate a large group. We were not invited to use them.

After the guided tour — which is not long — we elected to not explore other caves, though there are several that visitors can enter, and where the flashlights are really needed. For these caves, you're on your own, without guides.

If you're done for the day, retrace your route past Tule Lake and into Oregon. Once in Oregon, follow the signs to Medford and then to Ashland.

Shasta Caverns

Directions: Take I-5 south out of Ashland to Shasta Lake. Then follow the directions to Shasta Caverns posted on highway signs.

These are farther south than the Lava Beds, and you get to them by driving south on I-5 to Shasta Lake/reservoir. When you are in the area, there are signs advertising the caves and directing you to where the tour begins. You start by taking a short boat ride across a narrow part of Shasta Lake. This is one place mentioned in this book that we've never visited. We've house-boated several times on Shasta Lake, so have come near it. These caves are on my "to-do" list. I mention them here only to let you know that if visiting caves is something you like to do, it's here and available for your visit.

While Shasta Lake is in the northern part of Northern California, visiting the Shasta Caverns could be a long enough trip that you might want to devote a full day to the visit (including the round-trip drive from Ashland). I-5 highway leading to the lake is a very lovely drive, with beautiful vistas and inviting picnic areas, and it's worth the trip if your home base is from north of Ashland. If you live south of Ashland, you drive right by it and might like to plan a stop on the trip home.

To return to Ashland, follow I-5 north.

Covered Bridges

There are several covered bridges remaining in Oregon. Why were they built?

According to a pamphlet available through AAA, the reason was economic. Steel for bridge construction was scarce, but wood — particularly Douglas fir — was readily available. Yet, wood had a way of deteriorating rather quickly, so to prolong their lives, engineers put roofs over the wooden bridges. They continued to be built into the 1950's. (There's a small book, *Oregon Covered Bridges,* by Bert and Margie Webber, that gives additional information, including details of where the bridges are statewide and how to get there.)

If you like these historic structures — and I do — there are still a few you can visit within easy driving distance of Ashland. One AAA map shows where they are and gives a thumbnail description of each. Easiest to reach from Ashland are the ones listed in Jackson and Josephine counties.

Perhaps the closest — and certainly the furthest south — is **McKee Bridge**, open to pedestrians and bicyclists. Even though it's quite solid now, having been rebuilt in the 1990's, it does take upkeep. The local people near these covered bridges love their bridges. McKee Bridge enthusiasts recently raised money to make needed repairs to the roof and wooden plank approaches, and I suspect these volunteers will be out again raising money for their bridge as further repairs are needed. One of those recent volunteers was a descendant of the pioneer, Mrs. McKee, for whose family the bridge is named.

The structure crosses the Applegate River, and an added benefit of visiting this bridge is that it's in a lovely setting with picnic tables. Many families also enjoy wading or swimming in the river.

As mentioned, covered bridges need to be maintained, and many have not been, with the result that some have fallen or been closed or removed for safety reasons. In Southern Oregon, an example of a bridge that collapsed is the **Wimer Bridge** in the city of Wimer. It fell in 2003, and unfortunately, there were three pedestrians on the bridge at the time. Happily, while their injuries were significant, the people and their dog weren't killed and have since recovered.

After the bridge's collapse, Wimer residents and covered-bridge enthusiasts put their efforts into raising enough money to rebuild the structure. I was in the area about that time and visited the grocery store at the site. On display were a bumpersticker and a handcrafted cookbook (with local recipes) being sold to help pay for this building project. All the townspeople's efforts — along with Oregon State money — were successful, and the bridge has been rebuilt. It's now in full operation and still used by autos.

Other close bridges are **Antelope Creek Bridge** in Eagle Point and **Lost Creek Bridge**, near the small town of Lake Creek. Neither bridge is in its original location, but both are near it. Also, both are open to only foot and bicycle traffic. Antelope Creek Bridge now takes the name of its town (**Eagle Creek Bridge**) and closely parallels the newer concrete structure which replaced it. Windows were cut in the sides of the old bridge to provide better light. Once when we were walking across the bridge and admiring its construction, a deputy sheriff was also there leaning on the window ledge. He beckoned us over where he pointed out the spawning salmon beneath.

A block away is Eagle Creek's historic mill with its modern bakery.

The **Lost Creek Bridge** is a little more remote, off Hwy 140, and it appears rather fragile. At a length of 39 feet it has the distinction of being the shortest of Oregon covered bridges. Right beside the bridge is a small memorial park with a stage area — more a raised platform — and public restrooms. There are many small towns in Oregon, and Lake Creek is an example of how charming they can be!

There are many other covered bridges in Oregon. **Grave Creek Bridge** in Josephine County is near I-5 and is still in full operation. (Quite near it is a historic museum, small but interesting.)

On Hwy 42, the small town of Remote — about halfway between I-5 and Coos Bay — has a wonderful bridge. It was once called **Sandy Creek Bridge** because it crosses Sandy Creek, but now carries the name of its close neighbor, the town of **Remote**. At one time the highway — and consequently all traffic, including loaded logging trucks, crossed the bridge. As a result, design engineers used special trusses to provide extra support. The bridge now has a picnic table installed on it, right in the middle, and the area (which includes a large parking area and a port-a-potty) is a county park.

Farther north on I-5 **Cottage Grove lists five bridges** in or near its "city limits." So, if you're adventurous, hunt down your own favorite bridge. They're all over the state, from McKee (the most southern, though not near I-5) to Portland.

Directions on how the get to the mentioned bridges:

McKee Bridge – Drive through Jacksonville on Hwy 238. At Ruch, turn left onto Applegate Road. Watch for the small signs with arrows pointing to the left taking you up a sort of driveway. Beyond a small general store stands the bridge. Only pedestrians and cyclists can use this bridge.

Eagle Point Bridge – This bridge is in the city of Eagle Point. Leave I-5 at the Crater Lake exit (Hwy 62). Exit Hwy 62 to the right at Eagle Point. The bridge is at Main Street and Royal Avenue. No automobiles are permitted on this bridge.

Wimer Bridge –This is in the city of Wimer just before the Evans Creeks Road does an elbow turn to the left (when you're driving toward Medford). The bridge is to the right and you may drive over it if you wish. (Wimer isn't shown on some of my maps. For directions on how to get there, look on the chapter named *Small Towns*, pp. 89).

Lost Creek Bridge – You'll find this near the small town of Lake Creek, off Hwy 140. It's set back but viewable from the highway, and you can drive right up to it but not on it.

Grave Creek Bridge – This still-used bridge is off I-5 about 15 miles north of Grants Pass and viewable from the highway. Take the Sunny Valley exit from I-5 and follow the old highway to the bridge — perhaps a mile.

Remote – Hwy 42 passes right by Remote Bridge, which is about halfway between I-5 and Coos Bay.

A Day at the Beaches – Three Routes

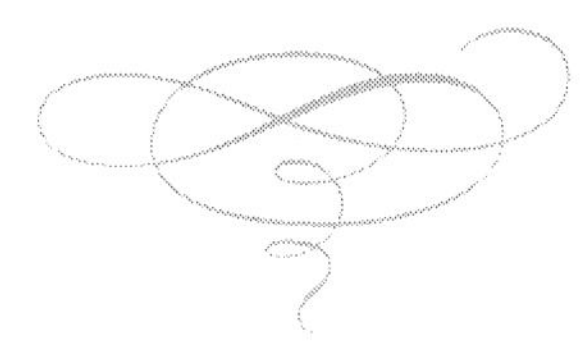

This is a full, long day of driving and activities. I've made this trip twice recently, once in May and the other in August. For the latter trip, we left Ashland around 7:15 a.m. and returned for a late dinner. Both trips took the route starting on I-5 and then taking State Highway 42 to U.S. 101 at Coos Bay.

The following several paragraphs describe what you see as you take this route to the ocean.

(**Note:** If your thing is to go to the beach, and just enjoy the sand and water — and sometimes the sun — you don't need this chapter. Drive directly to Coos Bay, aim north or south at Hwy 101 to whichever beach you prefer, pick your spot and enjoy. But if you're interested in the area and its inhabitants, stay with me.)

Starting from Ashland, the drive on I-5 to Hwy 99 is fast and beautiful, through rolling, forested lands. The cut-off through Dillard is narrower but scenic, following the Umpqua River. Dillard is a lumber-oriented town with huge warehouses and plywood manufacturing businesses. One area near the road is constantly being sprayed with water, and a sign factually warns of fog.

Turn left on to Hwy 42 at **Winston**. Winston, just south of the much larger Roseburg, is home to the Wildlife Safari, a drive-through 600-acre reserve where hundreds of wild animals roam free. I've discussed this attraction in the chapter named *Animals*, (pp. 119).

Stretches of Hwy 42, have been improved recently so you can take your time on smooth roads to savor the small towns and luscious scenery you pass through. There are recreation areas along the way, and you might see one you'd like to visit now or at a later time.

One treat on this stretch of road — at the appropriately named small town of **Remote** — is a clear view of Sandy Creek Covered Bridge, one of Oregon's many. (The bridge is also known by the name of Remote.) You don't have to make a detour off the highway to see it, for the bridge and its parking lot are right by the road. This well-preserved bridge no longer carries cars, but pedestrians can enjoy crossing the creek, just standing on it and gazing out the windows at the creek flowing by, or thinking about its previous use. (Did this bridge really once carry logging trucks?) You can also have lunch at a picnic table on the bridge. There's a port-a-potty nearby on the edge of the parking lot. The village of Remote has a rather large-sized school and a grocery store.

Continuing on Hwy 42, you pass **Coquille,** which is another lumber town and has large log ponds. It also has a theater — Saw Dust Theater — offering gay-nineties plays and olios, performed evenings from Memorial Day to Labor Day. Since we passed this town while on a day trip, we didn't have time to enjoy an evening theater experience; but this type of play is fun

— booing the villain and cheering the hero. Most of the productions we've seen of this type of play have been performed by amateurs where overacting is a virtue! Perhaps we'll try to include this sometime, for we have the impression that it's an ongoing attraction, offered every year.

Another "attraction" is a car wash for big rigs, trucks, and RV's. If you drive one of those vehicles, you might want to plan a stop here.

After leaving town the road follows **Davis Slough**, lined with frequent log pilings. We learned these were to protect the sides of the slough, helping guide logs and barges that float down this waterway. An interesting fact is that most of nearby Coos Bay is built on pilings, according to one native we chatted with.

Hwy 42 joins Hwy 101 just south of **Millington**, still another lumber town, before reaching the ocean at **Coos Bay**.

To get to the beaches the most direct way, before Coos Bay and after reaching the small town of Coaledo, look for the junction with Hwy 101 and turn left to drive south or right to head north.

Coos Bay

The Coos Bay area is alive with activity and commerce. There are industries regarding wood products (plywood, myrtle wood, etc.) and fish (including recreational and commercial fishing, canning, and exporting fish products), and a variety of recreational activities. The harbor at Coos

Bay has been dredged to accommodate the large, ocean-going freighters associated with exporting. There are several lovely state beaches and parks, and the drive along Hwy101 gives the tourist many views of outstanding rock formations and dashing waves.

Coos Bay is a combination of what was once three small towns, and it's now the largest city on the Oregon Coast. The Tourist Information Center provides a map of a self-guided walking tour of historic buildings in downtown Coos Bay. This tour would undoubtedly be interesting, especially to a history buff, and a welcome opportunity to get out of the car and stretch your legs. But if you have limited time, you could skip it or simply drive past some of the addresses shown on the map to enjoy taking a look at the turn-of-the-century (and earlier) architecture.

We stopped at a myrtlewood factory that offered daily self-guided tours. (There are many such factories offering tours in Southern Oregon.) We entered through the salesroom – where delicious fudge was for sale – and then we sat for a video presentation, which toured the working area, giving the basic information, then we were able to take a walk through the work area. Later we browsed the sales area and made a few purchases in the "seconds" section, where you can find items with only minor damage and greatly reduced in price. The salespeople were quite friendly and helpful.

On our first trip we discovered a charming city park for our picnic lunch. (Since it was foggy at the coast that day and sunny here, it was an easy decision where to eat!) The park is located at 10th Street and Commercial Avenue and is called Mingus Park. It has tennis courts street-side, and the development includes a large pond with a red Japanese bridge at one end. There are numerous ducks and geese in the pond plus a small island with a miniature lighthouse on it. There is a botanical trail (an asphalt path encircling the pond), which was being enjoyed by many townspeople "going for a constitutional." (When we were there, there was also a very friendly red-headed 10-year-old.) Many benches are sprinkled around the pond — fine for a simple picnic — and nearby there's a small play area with swings, etc., for young children. The park is well cared for, but the restrooms — at least when we were there — could use some sprucing up.

After lunch we aimed for the ocean, staying on small, unnumbered roads and enjoying the views. As mentioned before, from Coos Bay you can go north or south to enjoy ocean vistas, strolls on the beaches, or enjoy a little sun. Our most recent trip along the coast was foggy with rather mystical views of the sand and waves. We chose to go south through Charleston, then continue to Shore Acres State Park and Cape Arago State Park.

Charleston

Charleston is a fishing village, with boat-washing facilities, a dock with deep-sea-fishing charters, boat supply stores, a few restaurants, an oyster farm, and a motel. The village had a quaint feeling about it, reminding me a little of parts of Cannery Row in Monterey, California.

Leaving Charleston on the second trip we had not had lunch so we drove south and looked for a quiet place to picnic. We found the perfect location at Sunset Bay. If you travel with small children who might be intimidated by scary waves, you'll be delighted with this beach. The two sides of the bay nearly close its two arms, allowing only a small space for incoming waves. The result is a very pretty, very quiet introduction to the ocean.

Then continuing south a short distance we reached Shores Acres. Ah! It is so beautiful. This was our second visit, and we approached it with a kind of joy.

Shore Acres State Park

Shore Acres State Park is the former estate of a wealthy family, the Simpsons, who bequeathed this acreage to the state for a park, the Simpson's Botanical Gardens. There is a small observation building placed between the parking lot and the bluffs overlooking the ocean. Mounted on the inside walls of this little building are posters — large-captioned photographs of the Simpson houses that once stood here. There is also an audio presentation with information about the history of the family and the area.

Turning your back to the posters you look out through large windows facing the ocean. On a stormy day, this building would be a much-appreciated haven from which to observe the ocean. Our weather for both visits invited us out to walk along an asphalt path for a closer look at the waves smashing on boulders below us. (The paths are smooth and wide enough to accommodate a pushed wheelchair.)

Leaving the viewing area, we walked along a path (perhaps a hundred yards) through a densely wooded area, conifers and such, to where the path reaches a gate and opens dramatically into gorgeous formal gardens — well planned and superbly maintained. Mr. Simpson brought back some of these plants from his worldwide travels.

For us in both visits it was an "ah" and "ooh" moment. There are low hedges surrounding masses of flowering plants. To the right is a stretch of taller hedge, behind which is a lovely Japanese garden and pond.

Directly across the garden from our entrance to the formal gardens is an unpretentious wood-framed cottage. At first glance it looks rather small, but as you get close to it, you find it to be a fairly large house. This is one of the three houses that the Simpsons inhabited at one time or another and the only one still standing. It is not open to the public.

But what plants will you find in the garden? In the spring the largest part of the garden is ablaze with azaleas and rhododendrons of many colors. In the summer the same area shows off roses, perennials, and annuals in wonderful hues. There are continuous teams of gardeners busily at work, but they took time to answer our questions about the plants.

In addition to the gardens there are some services. In the gift shop, there are many garden-oriented items for sale and a staff of knowledgeable volunteers well qualified to answer questions both about the Shore Acres grounds and questions you might have about your own garden.

Back along the trail are drinking fountains and public restrooms, which are as well-tended as the gardens. Picnic tables are provided in secluded spots on the property outside the garden area.

We were not asked to pay an entrance fee, but I believe weekend guests are expected to do so. So come prepared to pay a fee but be pleasantly surprised if you don't have to do so.

For my family, this is such a satisfying place to visit that we plan to return soon!

Cape Arago

Leaving the Shore Acres State Park, we followed the road, which continues out to Cape Arago State Park. Overnight camping is prohibited, but there are picnic tables, public restrooms, and short hiking trails for day use.

And, of course, there are wonderful quick sights of the ocean.

At the end of this part of the road you come out to the cliffs and, finally, an unobstructed view of the waves. The trails take you to picnic tables on the cliffs and to the beaches below. It was too cool for picnicking here on this foggy day, but on a sunny day the vistas would provide a wonderful setting for lunch.

Swimming is discouraged for safety reasons. What's considered dangerous? The waters are habitually very turbulent, there's a strong undertow, and there are "sneaker waves," ones that sneak up unexpectedly on you. These waves make for impressive viewing from a safe distance of the cliffs, but are treacherous for swimmers.

The picnic areas are well laid out, and there are drinking fountains and trashcans. There's also one covered area with a barbeque pit and six tables lined up to accommodate a large group. Dogs are permitted only on leash. There are enough trails here to occupy a lot of refreshing time.

Bandon Area

Bandon is south of Cape Arago and has a lovely seafront with waves dashing up on its beach with its impressive rock formations. The village's history includes a few devastating fires — one in 1936 that destroyed nearly every building in town, so "Old Town" is a relative term.

The town has a good harbor but is better known as an artist colony, and it has some other attractions of interest, too. If antiques are your thing, you'll appreciate the few antique shops in town. In the Old Town area there's a sternwheeler that offers rides up the Coquille River. You'll also find a Cheese Factory. Since outside of town is an area of cranberry bogs, it's not surprising to find shops specializing in cranberries and related products. For instance there's a shop where you can watch cranberry sweets being prepared. There are also gift shops and art galleries.

The beach is known to be strewn occasionally with semi-precious stones such as agates and jasper, so it's not a stretch to find that beachcombing is popular. This sounds fun, so we're planning to spend more time beachcombing and exploring this inviting community.

Outside town just to the north is **Bullards Beach State Park**. Here there's a campground, picnicking (including another covered area for large groups), a children's play area, restrooms, and drinking water. Kite flying is popular here. There's also a horse-camping area where you can camp with your horse! The beach has light sand, and is long and wide, with driftwood and lots of space to walk and play.

The Coquille River Lighthouse is not out on the point, but nearby, inland on the riverbank. It's an attractive, octagonal structure, now used as an interpretive center. The lighthouse lens is no longer there, and access to the building is limited to the ground floor. There are nice views of the ocean from the windows. Hours are 10:00 a.m.-4:00 p.m.

Once while visiting the lighthouse, a couple arrived on horseback, and we had a pleasant conversation with them about their rescue horses (Mustangs). They were making use of the horse camping grounds.

Nearby, the Coquille River is crossed by a drawbridge that lifts to allow the entrance of taller boats, such as sailboats with a fixed mast. If you're there at the right time you could watch such a passage.

There are asphalt paths, separated from but parallel to the road, where we saw people walking their dogs or riding their bicycles.

Seven miles south of Bandon is a tourist attraction that should appeal to people of all ages, the **West Coast Game Park Safari**. It's a petting zoo, including many animals you don't normally see in petting zoos. The animals range from tigers and bears to sheep and goats, though the more dangerous animals never make it out of fenced areas. The one exception to this general rule is that baby animals in these "dangerous" families are sometimes brought out in controlled situations for you to admire their cuteness and cuddliness.

We found our visit there quite fun. It was certainly a wonderful time to get out and stretch our legs for about an hour. And watching the expressions on the faces of young visitors petting and seeing close-up some of these animals was part of the fun. There is an entrance fee. There's more information about our visit in the chapter on *Animals*, (pp. 123).

Return trip

We left Bandon area on Rt. 42S, cutting over to Rt. 42 at Coquille. Rt. 42S looks on the map as if it might be a dirt road, but it's paved — a good country road — going through pretty farmland and following the meandering river. It's not high speed, but since it cuts off several miles, it's a worthy route. Once on Rt. 42, we retraced our morning route back to Ashland.

Reflections

We stopped and chatted with people many times, took our time going through the Myrtlewood Factory, walked many provided trails — in short, had a leisurely day. It was very satisfying, but we returned about 8:30 p.m., ready for dinner and relaxing — too much and too long a day if we had evening theater tickets. So then, this thoroughly delightful trip would not combine well with an evening engagement.

A Day at the Beaches – Route #2

The second trip takes you through Grants Pass to Crescent City on Hwy 199, and takes less time than the route going through Coos Bay.

The first part of this route covers area we visited in going to Oregon Caves National Monument and Great Cats World Park. Once past those venues, the lovely road weaves through forested lands until reaching the California State line and then dips down into California to reach the ocean at Crescent City. Along the way the road passes several small towns, O'Brien having a service station and Gasquet (CA) including a market and a ranger station. The stretch of highway basically from the state line to Hiouchi, CA, follows the beautiful Smith River and is designated as a National Scenic Byway. (The beauty of this stretch of road is best enjoyed while driving northeast — the return trip — because then the pullouts overlooking the river are on your side of the road.) Between Hiouchi and Crescent City is **Jedediah Smith Redwoods State Park**, where you'll see seriously large trees, old growth Sequoia Sempervirens (Coast Redwoods). I live near Big Basin in California, which is one of a few state parks having these impressive trees and can remember many visits to enjoy their beauty. They're very tall — some over 300 feet high — and some grow 15 or more feet wide. A man who owned some property near Crescent City where one of these huge trees grew, carved a tunnel through one of them that was wide enough for a car to drive through. A few other people did this also. While perhaps an interesting experience to drive through a living tree, the trees didn't like it. (There's one such tree still standing in one of the Redwood Highway groves, elsewhere in California.)

Jedediah Smith Redwoods State Park includes most of the amenities expected in a state park, including camping, picnicking, hiking, boating, swimming, fishing, a visitor center, and restrooms (some of which are near the highway).

Just before Crescent City, which we'll visit on the way back, is a cutoff (Hwy 197) to the city of Smith River which shortens the trip a little, but basically saves the driver from navigating through the larger city with its traffic. You're soon back in Oregon with **Brookings** your first city. The city itself, with a population of over 5,000, has many of the large department stores, such as Fred Meyer, and numerous service stations and restaurants.

Probably because Brookings is the first city as you drive north, it has a very convenient and well-stocked and staffed Information Center. This is on the ocean side of the highway, roadside of a large shopping complex which has a few restaurants, gift shops, etc. It's very easy to get to and provides many helpful maps and pamphlets. The attendant we met was a longtime resident of the area and aimed us toward places we'd never considered.

One of the pamphlet/maps we found directed us to the only place along the Pacific Coast that had an aerial attack by the Japanese during World War II. It's located east of Hwy 101, beyond the large bridge that's viewable from the highway. Just before you cross it, turn to the left and proceed to Mount Emily Road. (I realize these directions are a little sketchy, but the pamphlet I picked up gave no directions on how to get there. The Information Center attendant could be most helpful.) Unfortunately, the site of the attack is some distance down a narrow dirt and gravel road. We just didn't have enough time to visit this historic place, but would like to in the near future. I'm not sure what we'll find, but it may have only a simple marker stating that this is where the incendiary device landed.

The attack came from a small plane assembled and launched from a Japanese sub that surfaced off the coast near Brookings. The pilot flew over forested lands nearby and dropped the device that was supposed to ignite on impact and start a forest fire. The plan was to cause panic among Oregon citizens. However, the woods were moist and only a small fire started which soon burned itself out, causing no significant damage. There is a museum a little further north on Hwy 101 that records the postwar visit of the Japanese pilot who dropped the bomb. He apologized for his part in the attack and presented some items to be included in the museum display, including his family's 400-year-old Samurai Sword. There's another museum (Pottsville in Merlin) that displays one of the devices that didn't work and was recovered. It doesn't look like a bomb.

One venue at Brookings, which has several activities of interest is **Azalea State Park —** east and adjacent to U.S. Hwy 101. Here in the spring and fall, you'll find more than 1,000 wild azaleas and rhododendrons blooming. Within this 27-acre park is also a nice children's play area called Kidtown with restrooms across the street. And nearby in the summertime there are concerts under the stars on the park's outdoor stage. A chapel with an intriguing design is around the corner from the stage area. Picnicking locations are available.

The temperature of Brookings is so mild that not only do azaleas bloom twice a year, but acres of flowers bloom year round; in fact, about 90 percent of the country's Easter lilies grow here. So this is a colorful place. You'll also find myrtle trees growing big and healthy here. Myrtlewood trees are said to grow naturally only in southwest Oregon and in Palestine.

Along this stretch of coast, the beaches are composed of darker and larger pebbled sand; and, particularly by Brookings, there are unusual rock formations near the shore, some of which are creatively named, such as Hunchback Rock and Humbug Mountain. Cape Sebastian, less imaginatively named, has a formation viewable for some distance. Other parks are named for formerly prominent people, such as Samuel Boardman, unknown to most of today's visitors.

Not surprisingly, Highway 101 north of Brookings is another stretch designated as a Scenic Byway, this one named for Cape Sebastian.

The ocean views are beautiful and many, and there are plentiful pullouts to beaches, so you can take pictures, get a better look at rock formations, or get your feet wet in the ocean. We found Battle Creek Historic Wayside and Arch Rock Point particularly interesting and attractive. But all along this part of the coast you can always picnic on the beach, make sandcastles, or indulge in other favorite beach activities.

A few other destinations of note are near **Port Orford,** named for British Earl of Orford around 1800. Along the highway is a tourist spot, the **Prehistoric Garden** where there are life-sized replicas of dinosaurs in a rainforest setting, peeking out from under and behind trees and shrubs. Some of the replicas are painted in surprisingly bright colors, and the park has received some criticism for this. But who knows? Those responsible for building the park with its replicas did a lot of research into the size and proportions of the beasts. Maybe they got the colors just right. Dogs are allowed, presumably on a leash. This venue is largely for children, but adults can enjoy it, too. We visited on a warm day and were pleased with the cooling shade. The hours vary with the time of year, and there's a fee. It is suggested that visitors call ahead to check the hours (call 541-332-4463). Partly educational and perhaps considered by some to be a bit hokey, it's a nice change from the miles of beaches and other beautiful sights.

Cape Blanco State Park is off Hwy 101, reached by driving four miles north of Port Orford, then west for three miles. This park houses the Cape Blanco Lighthouse, with tours Tuesday-Sunday, 10:00 a.m.-3:30 p.m., April-October. There's a small fee for folks over 15 years of age.

In the same park is the **Hughes House**, built in 1898, where the early pioneer Hughes family lived and worked. Tours are available, except on Mondays, so you can see how pioneers lived. There are photographs and a variety of antiques. In the valley below the house is the area they farmed. There is no admission fee, but donations are appreciated. It should take about 30 minutes to go through the house.

Port Orford also has a **Lifeboat Station Museum** at Port Orford Heads State Park on Coast Guard Road. The station operated from 1934 to 1970 and provided search and rescue assistance. The displays in this museum include a 36-foot motor lifeboat and a Lyle rescue gun. The park also has walking trails taking you out to views of the ocean. When I visited, the museum was open April-October. Check ahead at 541-332-0521 for the days and hours visitors may enter to see the interior displays. If your hours don't fit with theirs, you may be able to make an appointment for another time.

Like so many towns in this area there are ample fishing and day river trip possibilities. Forest and trail information is available at the

Gold Beach Ranger District 29279 Ellensburg Ave, Gold Beach, OR (541) 247-3600.

The next significant town north of Port Orford is Bandon, covered in the first "Day at the Beaches" section. So, from here, you can explore further north on your own or aim back to Crescent City.

Can you guess why Crescent City is so named? Why, because its beach is crescent shaped. A look at a California State map shows that Crescent City pretty significantly juts out into the Pacific, and big storms potentially hit it rather hard, and of course so do tsunamis. A large part of the city which you now see is really rather new because in 1964 a large portion of its historic past was destroyed by a tsunami, which resulted from the destructive earthquake in Alaska. More recently the harbor was damaged by the March 2011 Japanese tsunami. The damage to the harbor and wharf was significant, but the waves didn't harm the city itself.

Since Crescent City is very close to two large redwood parks, Jedediah Smith and Del Norte, visiting the redwoods is a primary interest of the city. (There is a Visitor Center, **Redwood National and State Parks Headquarters**, on 2nd Street in town, supplying maps and brochures describing the parks.) Before visiting Crescent City, we enjoyed a rather easy hike among the redwoods where we could admire these giant trees before the trail eventually took us to the river. Here, some people sat down to rest and sun themselves before returning to their cars in the parking lot. This is one of a few easy hikes among the redwoods the visitor can make, and such a walk is highly recommended.

Along Hwy 101 at the north edge of town is **Ocean World**, their aquarium. It's not nearly the enterprise of the one in Monterey, CA with its many well-planned exhibits. This one uses the gift shop as a waiting area for their tours. So, before the beginning of the tour, you're encouraged to browse the shop with its usual assortment of T-shirts, colorful trinkets, etc. But wait. The tour is worth the wait. Along the tour a guide gives factual information about the sea anemones, bat rays, and sharks you pass. These sea-creatures are in shallow elevated ponds made for easy petting – which the visitor is encouraged to do. All these sea-creatures are tame enough to do you no harm, so if you've ever wondered what a shark feels like, here is your opportunity.

But the highlight of the tour is the sea lion show. This is presented on an outside balcony, with some seals and the sea lion star swimming in a pond below you. This sea lion – Chloe – is a very remarkable animal. She's about a year old as of summer 2012, and has quickly learned over 30 cues to do tricks to entertain you. If you know anything about animals learning tricks, you know that these tricks result from behavior that the animals demonstrate on their own and are then incorporated into the act. Chloe acted as if she was having a wonderful time high-fiving, swishing, leaping, diving, retrieving, "barking," etc. for about 15 minutes. We plan to revisit Chloe – perhaps next year.

Crescent City has a working **lighthouse** on Battery Point Island at the end of H Street. It includes a museum which displays nautical memorabilia and such items as antique clocks and photographs of shipwrecks and lighthouses, both American and foreign. Guided tours are available. You can visit Wed-Sun, April-October, 10:00 a.m.- 4:00 p.m. only at low tide. If you want to check hours, call 707-464-3089.

This city is the jumping off place to stay if you're exploring the redwood forests nearby. There is a scenic 42-mile stretch of Rt. 199 that winds through the forests and along the Smith River that is well worth a leisurely drive.

Also in the area is **The Trees of Mystery**. Most of what you see along the walking paths is a bit hokey, largely from the names given to trees that have been misshapen by nature and have an intriguing look. But this place could be interesting to curious adults or to you with children.

Near the city limits are paved tracks that take you to lovely overlooks of the ocean. The Chamber of Commerce can provide maps and pamphlets.

We have had a favorite restaurant that overlooked the ocean. It may not be there still, but look for similar restaurants and enjoy a meal with a view before returning to Ashland.

The return drive follows the lovely Hwy 199 with many pullouts to admire the Smith River. Eventually you pass through Cave Junction, Grants Pass, on to I-5, and to Ashland.

Drive to the beaches – Route #3
This drive is for the experienced, capable driver.

Directions: Start on I-5 and exit to Merlin and Galice (highway exit 61) and then continue to Gold Beach. Travel south to Crescent City. Eventually return to Grants Pass via Hwy 199 and Ashland on I-5. This is about a 12-hour trip.

(**Serious Note:** Here's a warning. The following section of road from Galice to Agness is very scenic and included in this chapter for its beauty. Also without it you cannot complete this third route. However, for many drivers it has its drawbacks. We took this road under the direction and in the company of a ranger friend, who first ascertained if we were comfortable with narrow winding roads. Why? A Bureau of Land Management folder directs travelers to be cautious when driving this road, for most of this distance has only one lane to accommodate both directions. It does have frequent pullouts to allow traffic heading toward each other to pass, but remember that if you meet another vehicle while you're driving downhill, state law says you are the driver to back up to reach a pullout. And remember, too, that logging trucks, which frequent this roadway don't leave much room for other vehicles, even at the pullouts. Also, if you wish to drive faster than the car ahead of you, there's no room to pass unless the other driver is gracious enough to pull out into one of the spots so provided. Since this may not always happen immediately, you need to be patient.)

A final caution is: **don't even think about driving this in the winter.** The road is not plowed during the snowy season, and, in fact, the map indicates that it's closed during the winter. (I believe this is the road where, a few years ago, a young family got lost driving at Thanksgiving time at night in winter conditions. How they got onto a closed road I don't know. When they got stuck, the young husband tried to walk for help and lost his life, while his wife and two children were in jeopardy for several days before they were rescued.) Night driving would be challenging because not only are there no homes, businesses, or services near, neither are there street lights, nor are there rails at the edge of this winding road. If you want to drive this beautiful route, **do it on a summer day, and then only if you enjoy mountain driving.** End of warning.

To start this route, turn off I-5 just north of Grants Pass and follow the signs west to **Merlin**, the small town you passed through if you went to Wildlife Images. Beyond Merlin you'll be following the Rogue River and will pass several camping and picnicking places, of which **Indian Mary** is especially inviting. This is a small park owned by an Indian tribe and is considered to be a reservation, even in its small size. Open to the public, the picnic tables on well-kept grass near the river invite the visitor to stay for a meal. You can also notice the overnight accommodations in yurts, circular domed structures, which are offered instead of the typical motel.

Continue toward **Galice on Rt. 23**. The road is now called Galice-Hellgate National Country Byway and still has two lanes. There are trails if you choose to hike. Also, there are historic spots from time to time reminding one of the gold mining era. But largely, to quote a bureau of Land Management folder: the byway "extends high into the Siskiyou Mountains and offers broad and spectacular vistas of the Rogue River's rugged canyons." Here the scenery changes dramatically, with a transition to a deep river canyon having impressive rock walls bordered by forested slopes. This is rafting area, having many large places to park along the road, probably to accommodate the rafters. But it also encourages the driver to take his time and admire the scenery or perhaps at times to get down to river level and wade.

It's the section of road between Galice and Agness where it becomes only one lane. What started as good country road at Merlin becomes smooth, paved, narrow, one-lane road with frequent pullouts near Galice. The road is very scenic, winding through rolling forested lands and a rock-lined canyon. Occasionally, springs produce lush green growth in crevices behind bends in the road, and frequently the road opens up to grand vistas, tiers of distant blue mountains covered with old growth.

About 12 miles out of Galice is **Soldier Camp Saddle,** 3,569 feet elevation, the site of a devastating 1987 fire. A large sign gives the history of the lightning-started fire that destroyed 32,000 acres of wilderness forests, described as "lands never entered." But the destroyed acres have been replanted now, with ferns and manzanitas thriving beside young forest shrubs and trees.

At about 23 miles from Galice is **Bear Camp Summit** with a 4,319 feet elevation, which is the highest point of the drive. There's a pullout parking area, including a few picnic tables, where you can enjoy the wonderful vistas of the western side of these mountains. Since this is an infrequently traveled road, you won't be bothered by parades of cars.

Near **Agness**, you join Rt. 33, which is good, two-lane road, for the final 29 miles to **Gold Beach**. You cross the Illinois River, follow the Rogue River, and find smaller streams with colorful names, such as Nail Keg Creek.

Once at the ocean, you can explore **Gold Beach**, a former gold mining area until a big storm washed its riches out to sea. There are jet boat and Rogue River Mail Boat rides available in Gold Beach on the Rogue River. Beaches and recreational activities in the area are popular. Some folks enjoy just sitting on the beach and watching pelicans, sea lions, and whales (in season). When it's low tide there are starfish, sea anemones, and other creatures inhabiting the tidal pools. Gold Beach also has a historic museum.

After leaving Gold Beach, continue south to Crescent City and return to I-5 on Hwy 199.

Mt. Shasta along the ride. And then, somewhere along the way, a small group of bandits "held up" the passengers — riding horses and wearing bandanas over their faces like bad guys did in the Old West. It was rather hokey but fun.

And then, a few years ago, the owner of this venue disappeared — no one knows what happened to him — and the whole thing was put on hold. Every time we drive past we see the train sitting there collecting dust and wonder what will happen to it. There has been talk that the heirs would like to start the rides again. There are legalities to work out, but if the rides are revitalized, this would be a fun thing to do with children. The local Chamber of Commerce staff should be able to give you updated information.

The town of Yreka is interesting for its historic background. It was originally a Native American area, and later the town became famous when gold was discovered nearby. You can take a walking tour of a historic residential area. In this neighborhood are old houses, largely lovely, well-kept homes from a bygone era. These houses are not on stately grounds, but show what the community looked like 100 years or so ago.

Also, nestled among some gas stations near I-5 is a rather charming statue — better, a group of statues — of some miners panning for gold.

If you're looking for a place to picnic near Yreka, there's **Greenhorn Park** just out of town near Greenhorn Reservoir. (Signs that direct to the park can be found near the offices of the Klamath National Forest, on the frontage road west side of I-5.) At Greenhorn, by the parking area along the large, well-maintained grassy field, are picnic tables and a playground. Short hiking trails start here also. In the dry summer that means crossing a bridge and walking along the dry creek bed. Here you can visit a restored miner's cabin and see some miner's equipment. Unfortunately, these attractions have been lessened in their appeal by the natural process of age, weather, and neglect, plus graffiti villains leaving their initials and drawings. You can boat and fish in the reservoir, viewable from the picnic tables. The park has some trees, offering a bit of shade, and the restrooms (when we visited) were clean and well tended. In all, it is a nice place to stretch your legs and enjoy a repast.

In town at 311 Fourth Street, you used to be able to visit the old **Siskiyou County Courthouse** and see their display of various forms of gold. It was open 8:00 a.m. to 5:00 p.m. Monday-Friday, but closed on holidays. You'll notice I use the past tense. In early spring of 2012 the Courthouse was broken into and the collection of valuable and irreplaceable gold was stolen. I've been told the value was over a million dollars. Since the main part of the display is now missing, the people who make the decisions aren't sure what they're going to do. Perhaps they'll have artisans make replicas and re-open. Or perhaps they'll decide to close it all down. I don't know when they'll make a final decision, but it was a popular attraction, and I'm sorry I didn't get a chance to see it.

Another tourist attraction in Yreka, at 910 S. Main, is the outdoor **Siskiyou County Museum**, which includes displays about American Indians and fur trappers, and activities such as gold mining, logging and lumbering, and the military. The exhibits feature equipment and restored buildings in a mid-1800's mining and pioneering settlement. This sounds intriguing, and hopefully it will be better maintained than the smaller one in Greenhorn Park. It's on my agenda for the next trip I make to the city. It's suggested that you should expect to spend a minimum of two hours here. It's open Tuesday-Friday, 9:00 a.m. to 5:00 p.m.; and Saturdays 9:00 to 4:00 p.m. It's closed holidays. There is a fee.

Since schedules change, in all cases where the hours are stated, you should play it safe and check the times before you set your itinerary. The headquarters office of Klamath National Forest, at 1711 S. Main St. Yreka, CA, phone: 530-842-6131 can help you with hours, directions, and maps. I found them very friendly and helpful.

Mt. Shasta city

The dominating geological feature as you drive south is Mt. Shasta, with its year-round snow and glaciers. If you're a very serious hiker/climber there are trails up this dormant volcano.

The ranger station in Ashland, for one, should be able to give you any information needed before attempting this ascent. Since I'm not a climber I can't tell you about the delights of this climb, but I do understand that this is not a casual walk for the inexperienced. Apparently, this is more a climb than a hike.

The **city of Mt. Shasta** is at the foot of the mountain, near Black Butte, the cinder cone near I-5. The city is not a metropolis, but it has several streets of businesses, including restaurants and grocery stores, plus an Information Center, which is advertised on street signs. The attendants are knowledgeable and friendly.

Mt. Shasta and Dunsmuir, a few miles down I-5 (both discussed in *Rivers and Falls*, pp. 179) have lovely waterfalls. Unfortunately, when we were there workers were reconstructing trails, plus we had limited time, so we chose Hedge Creek Falls. This visit is explored under the city of Dunsmuir.

The other place of interest, which we visited, is Mt. Shasta's city park — rather large and shaded — with buildings having meeting rooms. Outside are picnic tables, some of them to accommodate large groups. As we walked past one such group, several folks smiled and waved.

But most importantly the park is the home of the headwaters of the Sacramento River. The source of this mighty river is a group of three springs located close to each other, which gush out a lot of water. The water flows into a sort of swampy area, which you can explore on paths crossing and re-crossing this swamp before the water becomes a stream and eventually the river. In the area near the swamp, you can cross the Sacramento in a big step. (A few miles away you need a large bridge.)

But how exciting for me! I have strolled the few feet over the beginnings of thee mighty rivers: the Mississippi River in a different state at a different time, the Rogue River just a few days before, and now the Sacramento.

Later down Hwy 101 the now large river flows in and out of Shasta Dam, and the highway crosses it several times before it reaches Sacramento, the state capitol. From there it empties out into the San Francisco Bay.

Going back to the springs, apparently the water is rather pure and sought after, for there were people lining up to fill jugs with this water for their personal use. We lined up and tried it, too, and were glad for the fresh, cool water. You may wish to bring a jug if you go here.

Lake Siskiyou

This little jewel is just south of Mt. Shasta city and on the west side of I-5. You can get there by staying mainly on county roads rather than going on I-5 for such a short time. Before heading out, ask at the Information Center and get a map.

The lake reminded me of the Alpine-like lakes in Southern Oregon — Hyatt and Howard

Prairie Lakes, etc. Evergreen trees come right to water's edge, and the water is crystal clear. When we were there, a few people were lazing on small boats or the beach area, and the lake and surroundings were calm, cool, and inviting.

Dunsmuir

Dunsmuir is about the same size as Mt. Shasta city, and also inhabited by friendly people. Have you heard of the Dunsmuir train disaster that occurred several years ago? (The national media publicized details for days if not weeks.) There was a railroad accident that included the derailing and tipping over of freight cars, with the result of a devastating toxic spill. All wildlife in or near the water were killed, and the water was contaminated for years. But now the water is safe, and wildlife has been restored.

Dunsmuir has a city park and a lovely waterfall, Hedge Creek Falls, which we visited first. (See the chapter *Rivers and Waterfalls,* (pp. 179), for directions on how to get there.) This waterfall is not only very pretty, but its spray is most welcome on a warm day. The trail actually leads you behind the fall, but you don't get really wet — just cooled down. If you want to combine enjoying the fall with a hike, continue on the trail on the other side of the stream for a short distance before you retrace your steps and return to the car.

For a lovely added stop in Dunsmuir, stay on North Dunsmuir Road and follow the signs to their city park, with it's small but lovely botanical garden. The gardens and children's play area are mostly under large trees and offer pleasant shade. Spread out among the shrubs and flowers are several statues of children doing things kids do – for instance, one playing with a pet and another lying on his stomach.

The entrance road takes you right to a parking lot with many spaces. In addition to the gardens are picnic tables, tennis courts, and playing fields. There's also a short trail to fishing. (We talked to two happy fishermen who proudly exhibited their catch of two or three large trout they had just caught.) Nearby is a monument providing some history about early residents. Adjacent to the gardens are public restrooms.

If you just want to explore a bit of Northern California, you could enjoy most of the above-described destinations in a few hours. Quality time at Lake Siskiyou would take more time, but from this point on, even just to explore, you might want to spend the better part of a day.

Castle Crags

About six miles further south on I-5 and again on the west side of the highway is Castle Crags, a large outcropping of granite on the hillside. It has 4,350 acres of state recreation area. (The Crags are viewable heading south, but the better view is when you're heading north.) A road takes you to the top of the Crags where there is an assortment of offerings: camping, picnicking, trails to hike or ride (including both nature trails and horse trails), boating, swimming, fishing, etc. There's a visitor center. Pets on leash are allowed. From the top, vistas along the trails look out over the surrounding forest. (A motel featuring "rooms" of retired railroad cabooses is below the Crags in the area along the highway. It's not connected to the recreation area, but if you don't want to camp, it's an interesting place to spend a night.)

Shasta Dam and Lake

The drive south from Dunsmuir to Shasta Lake is very beautiful. Drivers too often are in a hurry to get from wherever to wherever and don't appreciate how beautiful the scenery is. The highway gently winds through evergreen stands of trees and eventually to several views of the lake. Shasta Lake was created to provide water for agriculture, but its main use has become recreational such as water-skiing and fishing, from boats and along the shore.

But first, an activity you can do in a reasonably short time is to explore the dam itself. In the visitor center there are large pictures on the wall showing the construction and uses of the dam. A 30-minute video about the area is shown throughout the day, and short-guided walks are also available. There's a parking lot for cars.

What about boating on the lake? Some folks own and dock their own houseboats or motorboats here. Alternately, several companies provide these boats for short time rentals — for a few days, a week, or longer. There are even a few day-rentals of covered craft that float but that's about it — no amenities such as kitchens, restrooms, or beds.

My family has rented houseboats several years for a few days at a time and remembers our stays at the lake among the most restful vacations we've taken. The boats travel at modest speeds, which enable you carefully to explore many nooks and crannies along the lake edge. When you find an interesting place, the "pilot" turns the craft toward the shore and beaches it. Once the front end is fairly secure, someone jumps out (usually into shallow water) and ties up with the rebar stakes and ropes provided. Tying up successfully is an art, but sleeping with the gentle movement of the water is very soothing.

Since we're talking about day trips most of the activities here are out of the question. But you may want to plan a few extra days some year.

Redding

It may be stretching it a bit to include Redding in a day's outing, but if you're vastly interested in sundial bridges, they have one. The bridge crosses the Sacramento River and is visible from I-5 if you know where to look. State Hwy 44

East goes to Mt. Lassen. Hwy 44 West goes into Redding at Turtle Bay, and this is where you find the Sun Dial Bridge. The bridge surface is translucent and is mostly a foot bridge, though service pick-up trucks use it, too. On the far side of the bridge is the series of stones that enable you to tell time — where the shadow of the "mast" on the bridge falls.

Also on this far side of the river is a nice, well laid-out botanical garden. On one visit a favorite spot was a house-like area where a couple of large vines comprised the structure; there were doors and windows where you could enter/exit or look out.

There is a fee to enter the gardens.

Also in the city is a sculpture garden, located on the grounds of the city hall. Here is a rotating display of sculptures of many artistic styles. There are benches where city folk sit to contemplate the art works or their thoughts. Oh yes, when we were there we were in the company of a number of Canadian geese. There is no fee to visit this area.

From this point either head back to Ashland or continue to your destinations in California.

If you're heading back to Ashland, you'll see signs directing you to **Lake Shastina** near Weed. I've wanted to explore this lake for years. Since it's near Mount Shasta I had visions of cool, crystal clear water and evergreen trees. Wrong. When I finally visited, I'm afraid my reaction was that once I'd visited the lake I didn't ever need to do it again. It's rather barren with few if any trees!

And on the hot day I was there being wet didn't decrease the feeling of heat. There were a few good things. At the main part of the lake there's a good boat ramp and fine restrooms. A few miles away there's a campground, though that, too, looked dry and hot. Certainly, there are many residences not far from the lake plus a nice golf course, so on cooler days the whole ambiance may be different. But my perhaps snide remark is, "Visit it if you must." Sorry.

Mt. Lassen

I mentioned Mt. Lassen a few pages back. It would definitely be too much to include a visit to this park in a one-day outing because there are so many interesting things to do. But permit me to digress briefly and describe this National Park.

More properly Mt. Lassen belongs to North Central California, being the southern end of the Cascade Mountains. But the easiest way to get there is from I-5. So if you want to plan on a visit at a later date, Redding is a good place to start. The park provides a motel accommodation, but there are other housing opportunities nearby, outside the park.

Directions: Take Hwy 44 from I-5. This road goes directly to **Lassen Volcanic National Park**.

The park is very interesting and educational, with many nature trails. If you want to learn about volcanoes, this would be a good place to visit. Roads and trails encircle the points of interest, so a disabled person could get close to the action. There are several lovely lakes, some of which provide fishing opportunities. Also, there are a few smaller volcanoes within the park. There are trails going up the Cinder Cone and skirting fumaroles, leading right up to pools of bubbling mud and boiling water. The fragrance of sulfur hangs heavy in the air.

There's no doubt that Lassen is an active volcano, but it's not dangerous. It last erupted in 1921 and hasn't burped since — hasn't displayed those active features that warn an eruption is near. Mother Nature always gives notice. If rangers in any of the parks having volcanoes become aware of an impending eruption, they warn visitors to leave, and leave you must! But folks always have a couple of days (not several minutes or hours) to get a safe distance away.

North of Lassen National Park on Hwy 299 is the town of Burney. Leaving Burney on Hwy 89 and driving about six miles you find **McArthur-Burney Falls,** a spring-fed fall nearly 130 feet high. If you find yourself in the area, this is a lovely sight, reached by a short walk.

I've finished my digression, so let's get back to places nearer to Ashland.

North Central California

Leave Ashland on Hwy 66 following directions to Klamath Falls. As with many drives in this part of the world, the road takes you through very pretty scenery — forests at first and then more barren volcanic land. The main destinations in North Central California are Tule Lake, Lava Beds, and Lower Klamath Lake.

To get to both Tule Lake and the Lava Beds, you take the same road, the Lava Beds being just a few miles further along the road. Inside Lava Beds National Monument are lava tube caves you can explore.

Directions: Leave Ashland on Rt. 66 to Klamath Falls where you look for State Hwy 39 (which becomes California 139 at the border). Once in California, at the small town of Tule Lake, watch for signs to the right that say either Tule Lake or Lava Beds. Following these directions you soon come to a stop sign at a T in the road. Turn to the left — you're now heading south — and after a mile or so you find Tule Lake Visitor Center on the right. The building is clean and modern, with displays including very lifelike "statues" of local birds and animals — not surprising since this is a wildlife refuge. The staff is helpful and interested in their subject.

There are picnic tables and a shady parking lot in addition to clean restrooms. Make use of all the above for there are no amenities or shade at the lake. Once you turn off the two-lane highway onto the dirt roads of the sanctuary, start looking for wildlife. We saw lots of birds, including several mama ducks leading their babes in what must have been their early swims. At different times of year you see a changing array of birds. If you're a "birder," you'll know what to expect. Otherwise, just enjoy nature's display.

This area is quite different from the lakes of Southern Oregon and those in western Northern California, for there are few trees here and this large lake is a fair distance from close proximity to the mountains. The mountains and lake seem to be pinkish. It's a different type of beauty, having its own kind of serenity. And the area, even though there are few trees to provide shade, is not dry and arid.

In a few additional miles south, the landscape becomes very rocky, with large, black, rough boulders, reminding us that we're now in volcanic country. We soon drove through the gates and past the entrance booth of the Lava Beds National Monument. Inside the Monument are the lava tube caves you can explore. There is a fee for proceeding.

This interesting Monument is discussed in the chapter named *Caves,* (pp. 205), because that's what the tubes are now. When you've finished exploring here, retrace your drive to Klamath Falls.

Lower Klamath Lake

The road to Lower Klamath Lake and its adjoining Wild Life Refuge is reached through Oregon. We were advised that this lake is rather marshy and not particularly pretty. It's interesting mostly to a dedicated birder. So, for you birders, to get to Lower Klamath Lake, drive to Merrill from Klamath Falls on Hwy 39. Merrill is a small town, so look for signs to the lake when you enter town. You'll be traveling a gravel road to somewhere near the lake, apparently not right up to the shore. Preparation? If you're birding for the first time, wear walking shoes, and bring your hat, bird book, and binoculars. Enjoy!

Places of Historic Interest

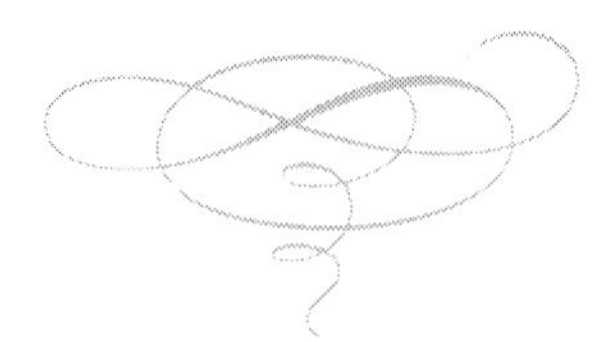

Southern Oregon and Northern California have many places of historic interest. Nearly every city has some statues, parks, or museums recalling the early days, some of which are mentioned throughout this book. Below are just some of the places that are perhaps mainly focused on history.

Jacksonville

The whole downtown of this Gold Rush community is a registered historic landmark. Most of the buildings date to the late 1800's and are well preserved. There are up-to-date modern businesses in many of them — such as a quilting shop — and others that mirror businesses of olden times — such as a fountain where you can buy a drink of sarsaparilla. The visitor is invited to stroll down the sidewalks of the few blocks comprising the downtown, observing or visiting the shops.

One old business is now a museum — one you can see into but not enter. This building is Beekman Bank at 3rd and California streets. Behind a glass wall are the furnishings just as they were in 1915 when Beekman died, furnishings dating from 1863 when the bank opened — the second bank in Oregon. Part of the room displays equipment used when gold miners brought in their ore for weighing and processing. Outside the backdoor and underground — with a transparent covering — are the underground pipes, etc., dating from pre-1915. A sign explains this display.

In the chapter on *Jacksonville*, (pp. 73), several other places of interest are mentioned.

Gin Lin Mining Trail

This very short trail winds through an area mined by a gold miner of the 1800's. You can see traces of different methods of gold mining. For more information about this trail see the chapter *Sports – Hiking*, (pp. 133).

Kerbyville Museum

Kerby is located on Highway 199 near Cave Junction. There is a lot in this museum, much of which is well displayed in glass cases. (Some items of clothing are on manikins.) Photographs that are decades old record early buildings and pioneers who settled the area. Gold panning is depicted, as are interplays with Indians. There are several musical instruments, guns, tools, and spaces showing a telephone operator at work and a country store displaying what a store would have sold 100 years or more ago.

Outside this building are a few other buildings — a blacksmith's workspace, a barn, and Oregon's only remaining one-room log school house. This school building is in such poor condition that entrance is not allowed, but you can look in from a safe distance. There's talk of shoring it up so that it's safer.

Brookings

On Hwy 101 on the coast, Brookings is the most southern of Oregon's coastal communities.

Brookings is the site of the only aerial attack on mainland USA by the Japanese in WWII. The site is just east of town near Mount Emily. The Chamber of Commerce in Brookings can provide pamphlets about this site and perhaps give you a map to the monument located where the attack occurred. It's an interesting story of how the Japanese accomplished this attack without flying in on airplanes. Instead, they managed to get submarines near the coast, surfaced, and quickly assembled and released a small plane carrying the munitions. There was no major damage because the grass and shrubs were so moist that no fire could get started.

While you're here, enjoying things historic, take pleasure in the ports and beaches along the way. Hunting for agates on the beaches is a popular activity. You can also go crabbing. Goat Island (also known as Bird Island), on the north end of Brookings, is a bird sanctuary, so if you're a "birder" bring your binoculars. State parks Harris and Loeb provide picnic areas.

Brookings also is the site of Azalea Park. If you're here in spring or fall you could see up to 1,000 wild azaleas and rhododendrons blooming. These plants thrive in the ocean-moist atmosphere and Brookings' mild climate.

Fort Klamath

Directions: On Hwy 62 north of Lake Klamath is the small town of Fort Klamath. Just south of town is the fort. To get there take the road to Crater Lake and continue south and east to Fort Klamath. Or Take Hwy 66 to Klamath Falls and drive north on the east side of the lake. (This is Hwy 97.) At the north end of the lake Hwy 62 branches off to the northwest. Drive to Fort Klamath.

In the middle of fields now dedicated to cattle raising are the remains of Fort Klamath. The fort was built in 1863 as an army post to protect wagon trains from attacks by Indians. There's a small museum, which pictures frontier life and includes Indian and army artifacts. Also on the grounds is a historic Post Office. Living history enactments featuring mock battles are presented a few times a year. (The information I have is unclear as to when these enactments take place. We arrived only to find the fort closed and locked. So if this place interests you, it is suggested that you should call and check the hours. The number is 541-381-2230 or 541-883-4208.) Visitors should allow one hour to enjoy this venue.

The fort is open only Thursday-Monday, 10:00 a.m.-6:00 p.m., June through September. Donations are welcome.

Applegate Trail Interpretive Center

Directions: This museum is off Hwy I-5 at exit 71.

This interpretive center is in a log building and is right by Grave Creek Covered Bridge. You can see the bridge from I-5. In the parking lot are some examples of covered wagons. Once inside the building, the host shows you a short video and orients you to what the museum includes. Then you're free to wander through the exhibits, which include a diorama and several displays showing how early settlers lived and how they dealt with Indian encounters and tragedies due to disease. While the museum isn't large, it's interesting and well kept.

North of the Interpretive Center, on I-5 at exit 76, is **Wolf Creek Inn**, another historic spot. It was built in the early 1880's as a stagecoach stop. The inn has been refurbished and the rooms are furnished to represent different periods when the inn was entertaining stage coach riders. You can take self-guiding tours through the inn and then exit to read the historic signs and paintings in front of the building. Also, if you time it right you can take a meal at the inn. That would be Thursday-Sunday, 9:30 a.m.-5:00 p.m. If you prefer to picnic, there's a small park with picnic tables and campsites nearby.

Yreka, California

Directions: Take I-5 south to Yreka.

There are several places under the heading of Yreka in *Northern California*, (pp. 252), that deal with history. There are two museums — Siskiyou County Courthouse and Siskiyou County Museum — plus Greenhorn Park. All three have displays dealing with gold mining and early pioneer days. The museum additionally tells of American Indians, fur trappers, logging, and lumbering. As mentioned before, following a devastating burglary, it is uncertain when or if the Courthouse will reopen.

In summary, if you want to become educated in a variety of historic events or eras, many opportunities await you.

Wineries

There are many wineries in Southern Oregon, and almost all of them offer tours and tasting opportunities.

One brochure says you can sniff the barrels and meet the winemakers.

Different parts of the state have growing conditions of climate and soil that are considered pretty ideal for certain wine grapes. One article on the subject lists the following grapes grown in warm Southern Oregon: Cabernet Sauvignon, Merlot, and Syrah.

Since I don't drink alcoholic beverages, I haven't visited any of the wineries. As a result I can't recommend any in particular; but we've driven past several that are nicely landscaped and look inviting. Does the landscaping have anything to do with the taste of the wine? It does show some attention to detail and displays a more welcoming appearance.

If wine tasting is your thing, there are several opportunities near Ashland. The phone-book Yellow Pages lists a couple of tours and a list of about 20 wineries. The web would also be a source of information.

Food

Food is a favorite subject with a lot of people, so let's talk about it.

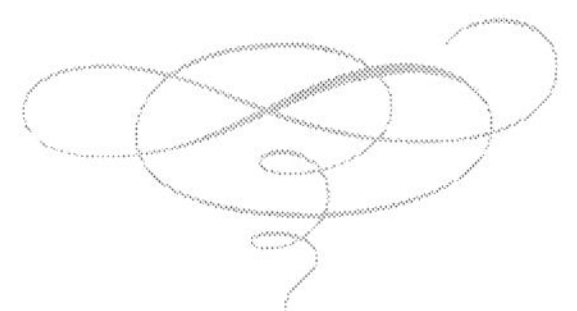

Am I going to list some of my favorite restaurants? Yes, but the places making this list are mainly for dinner.

First, let's start by talking about breakfast. I try to stay at a motel/hotel that provides a full continental breakfast where I can eat as much or as little as pleases me and where I don't have to place an order and wait for my meal to arrive. Another alterative my family has practiced is to travel with simple breakfast supplies and eat in our room. As a result, since I don't go to restaurants for breakfasts, I can't make any recommendations for this meal.

Secondly, as far as lunch is concerned, most days we're out and doing, not near a restaurant, so we picnic a lot. An exception to this practice is Sundays when we always have a lovely brunch at the **Winchester Inn** on 2nd Street in Ashland, where the food and service is wonderful, even memorable.

Why picnic? The advantage of a picnic is that it gives you lots of freedom. You can drive to a variety of desirable locations and not worry about when and where you're going to eat. Many places of destination provide picnic tables, but don't always provide a restaurant. (Since the tables may not be as clean as I prefer, I travel with a plastic tablecloth. Also we sometimes set up lunch in the back of our van and sit in our own shade, keeping pretty cool, even on warm days.)

What do we do for picnic food? If I don't want to prepare it myself, there are alternatives. There's a restaurant in north Ashland — the **Breadboard** at 744 North Main — that specializes in sandwiches. These are the hearty, substantive type, very delicious. Additionally, there's a **Subway** branch on Siskiyou Blvd. near the University. Both of these places wrap their products to go. Also the **Safeway store**, a block from the firehouse on Siskiyou Blvd., provides sandwiches and salads for take-out. Many Ashland restaurants are happy to pack a take-out.

When I prefer to make my own picnic, there are local grocery stores that provide whatever I need. Ashland has two large chain grocery stores, Safeway plus **Albertson's** on Ashland Avenue (also called Hwy 66) near I-5. I travel with a few basics plus a small ice chest to carry the meal.

Now, finally, where are some places we enjoy for dinner? As you've noticed, there are many places to eat in downtown Ashland — some of them have only a few tables. Many of these we haven't sampled, but the following establishments have been good enough that we've returned to enjoy other dinners. Let me make some general comments and then list the restaurants in alphabetical order.

We've been dining in Ashland for more than 30 years, and I can't be sure that the place we enjoyed one year will be there or be as wonderful the next visit. The restaurant may have gone out of business or may have hired a new chef with a different recipe for an old favorite. All the places I list are places we've visited at least once, except as noted. **Reservations are always a good idea.** Those restaurants located near the Festival usually provide excellent service, since they know the importance of making "the curtain" on time, but always politely tell them if you have time constraints. If you're in a real hurry you can speed up the ordering process by pre-choosing your meal by checking the menu posted outside the entrance. When your waiter arrives, place your order instead of asking to see a menu.

In all cases the accepted dress code is casual with shoes expected.

$ – up to $10
$$ – up to $20
$$$ – up to $30
Prices are subject to change.

1. **$$ – Alex's** – upstairs on the Plaza – Variety American cuisine.
2. **$$ – Black Sheep** – upstairs on the Plaza. (This has a funky pub atmosphere.) Our family gave the food mixed reviews.
3. **$ – Breadboard Restaurant** – 744 N. Main Street. Sandwiches and fresh baked goods. Also serves breakfast.
4. **$$$ – Callahan's** – 10 minutes from Ashland, at the I-5 exit to Mt. Ashland. We haven't

eaten here since it was rebuilt following a disastrous fire. Before the fire, "Mom" was the chef, and the cuisine was Italian, but it's different now – the building is prettier and the menu has changed and is more expensive.

5. **$$ – Dragonfly Café** and garden – 241 Hargadine Street, next to the Cabaret Theater. International Fusion cuisine.
6. **$$ – Greenleaf Restaurant** – 49 N. Main Street – on the Plaza. You can eat inside with air-conditioning or outside in back if there's table space. Variety American cuisine.
7. **$$$ – Larks** at Ashland Spring's Hotel – 212 Main Street. Variety American cuisine.
8. **$$ – Macaroni's Ristorante** – 58 E. Main Street – downstairs from Martino's. Italian cuisine plus salads and pizza.
9. **$$ – Martino's** – just off the bricks by Bowmer Theater – Italian cuisine plus salads and pizza.
10. **$ – Mihama** (Teriyaki and Grill) – 1253 Siskiyou Blvd., across the street from the University campus. Simple Teriaki cuisine plus chicken and hamburgers.
11. **$$$ – Omar's Steak and Seafood** – 1380 Siskiyou Blvd. This is beyond the University campus. Steak and seafood. Will prepare low-fat and low-cholesterol meals.
12. **$$ – Standing Stone Brewing Company** – 101 Oak Street. Wide variety including seafood, chicken, and pizza.

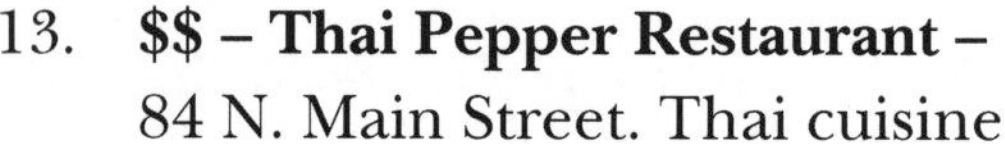

13. **$$ – Thai Pepper Restaurant –** 84 N. Main Street. Thai cuisine
14. **$$$ – Winchester Inn –** 35 S. Second Street. We eat here only for Sunday brunch (for about $15). We saw dinner menus, and the prices were higher. It has a lovely ambiance.

All these places are in Ashland. Fast-food chains like McDonald's and Wendy's are beyond the University, either on Siskiyou or on Hwy 66.

$$ – In Jacksonville is our favorite place to eat, but it doesn't fit with an evening Festival production. It's **The Jacksonville Inn –** 175 California Street between 3rd and 4th. It has the BEST FOOD, a pleasant wait staff, and a very pleasant outside dining area

Where to Get Additional Information

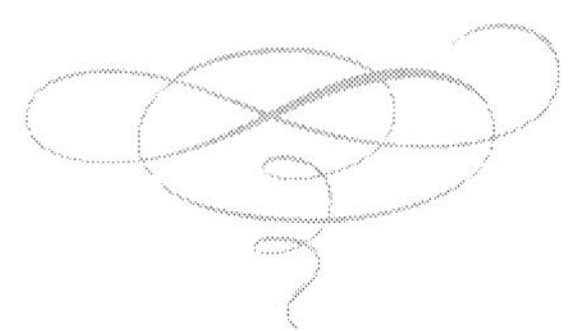

Obviously, you can look up information on-line, but beyond that here are some ideas.

1. If you're an AAA member, there's an office in Medford at 1777 E. Barnett Road, 97504. They're open Monday through Friday, 8:00 a.m. to 5:30 p.m. Other offices we've noticed are at Grants Pass, Coos Bay, and Klamath Falls. This is an excellent source for maps and accommodations.

2. Information Centers are available in several locations, where you can get pamphlets and maps for many tourist attractions. These centers are staffed by knowledgeable local people who are happy to answer your questions, share helpful information, and show you which pamphlets will meet your needs. I've visited Information Centers in Ashland (downtown adjacent to the Festival's Black Swan Theater), in Medford (adjacent to Harry and David's Country Store), and in Jacksonville (at North Oregon and C Street).

3. Ranger stations are a good source for maps and information about hiking trails, fishing, hunting, or the local countryside. If there's a roaring forest fire in the area, they can give you an update on the process of extinguishing the blaze or the wisdom of visiting a nearby location.

These stations are staffed by rangers who speak from experience; many of them actually get out and hike the trails, etc. Do check with them about the hunting season if you plan to hike in forested lands. The ranger stations can be found not only in forests but also in some towns. Ashland has one on Highway 66 near the Arco Station by the entrance to I-5. It's on the right side of the road (as you head toward I-5), and there's a small brown directional sign. We've also found ranger stations not far from McKee Covered Bridge near Ruch (Star Ranger Station) and another one near Prospect on the way to Crater Lake. Incidentally, these stations, open only Monday through Friday, have been a source of good restrooms, including those accommodating wheelchairs.

4. In Ashland there's a helpful store, named The Northwest Nature Store, on Oak Street, two blocks from the Festival. They stock a good selection of nature products and books. They also get out on the trails and can therefore answer a number of questions.

5. Telephone book Yellow Pages give helpful information. Most motel/hotel rooms or lobbies have one.

6. If you travel with a laptop or other electronic devices you can usually get good info on-line. However, I've found that the information

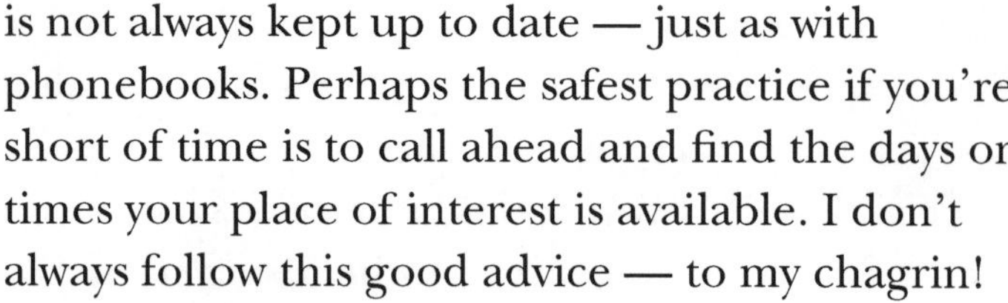

is not always kept up to date — just as with phonebooks. Perhaps the safest practice if you're short of time is to call ahead and find the days or times your place of interest is available. I don't always follow this good advice — to my chagrin!

7. Pay attention to roadside signs directing you to some attraction. Some of our very interesting stops have come about by this process.

8. Ask a friend, or the person you share a bench with at some venue, or ask a person you see taking pictures at some lovely sight. The possibilities are nearly endless of where to find helpful information. Find a common interest and ask where they've gone to see it. Adventures await you.

For Jim

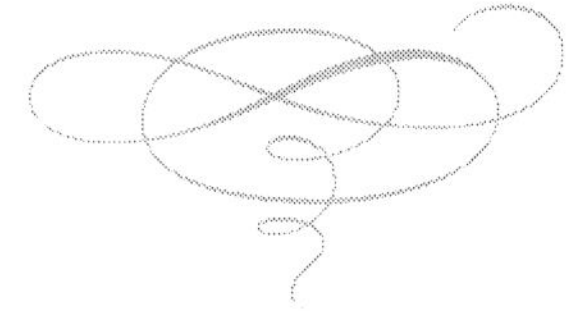

About the Author

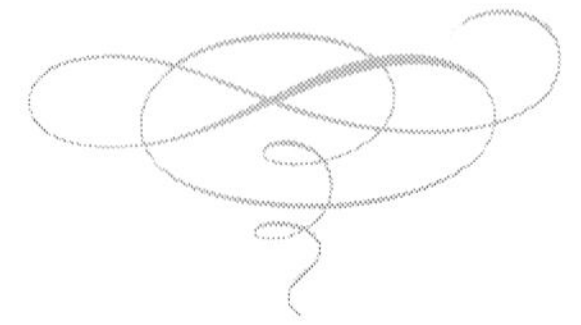

About Louise Hays Doolittle

Louise Hays Doolittle (Author) was born and raised in Palo Alto, CA, and earned her BA and MA at San Jose State University, with a major in Drama and a minor in English. She taught high-school English before taking a break to raise three children. Later she became an elementary school librarian.

Louise and her husband Jim bought a camper when their children were very young and spent their vacations exploring the USA. Along the way they developed a great appreciation for the wonders of nature. They visited all except six states, but their favorites were California and Oregon. They even branched out to house-boating on Shasta Lake.

Traveling almost automatically includes extensive picture taking. Gone are the 36 rolls of film tucked in a carry-all, and hello to the convenience of digital photography. Along the way Louise took some photography courses and now sells her pictures in note-card form.

In 1983 they accompanied an uncle to the Oregon Shakespeare Festival in Ashland, beginning a multi-decade love affair with both Shakespeare and Southern Oregon. Even though this uncle and Jim are gone now, Louise and daughter Patty still make annual trips to Southern Oregon and continue their exploration of this beautiful area.

About the Photographer

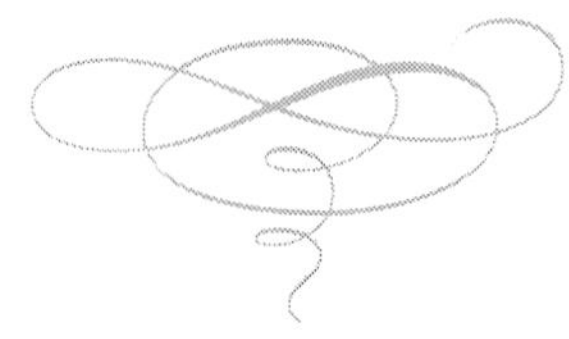

About Patty Doolittle

Patty Doolittle (photographer) has a B.A. in Art History, and has been interested in photography since she was given a camera at age 12. In addition to taking thousands of photos, Patty has also taken courses in Studio Art and Photography.

The middle child of Louise and Jim Doolittle's three children, Patty now lives in Palo Alto, CA, where she works in Administration at a local YMCA.

Patty's hobbies include gardening, painting, photography, dance and music. Her favorite animals are her cats. Her favorite activities are playing with her niece and nephew and traveling the world. Her favorite places to vacation are The Sea Ranch in Northern California, and of course, Ashland, Oregon.

Just for Fun

See if you can identify these pictures of places you might have seen in Southern Oregon.

Answers on page 298.

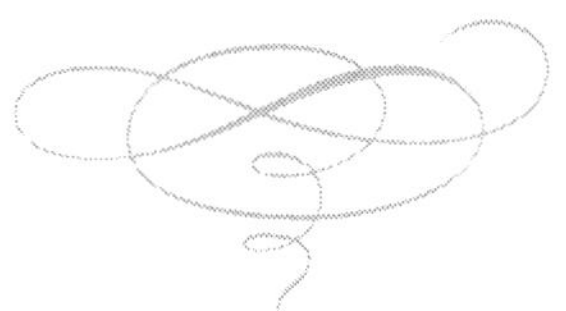

A

B

C

D

THE ROGUE VALLEY
Southern
Oregon
E

F

G

H

I

J

K

DON'T
EVEN THINK
ABOUT IT
L

M

N

Answers for "Just for Fun"

A. Rogue River bank temperature/time display
B. Jacksonville grocery store bird
C. Rotating dance statue on green in Lost Creek
D. Jedediah Smith Redwoods
E. Jacksonville trolley
F. Ashland Scienceworks Hands-on Museum wind apparatus
G. Cougar at Great Cats World Park
H. Agate Lake Park near Medford
I. Jacksonville underground display
J. City of Rogue River rooster
K. Ostrich welcomer at Wildlife Safari
L. McKee Covered Bridge — other side of river
M. Indian Mary Reservation totem pole
N. Statue at Dunsmuir, California, Botanical Park